My Child's Heart
Series #1

Let's Talk About Salvation

My Child's Heart
Series #1

Let's Talk About
Salvation

Kathy Kirk

Pleasant Word
A Division of WINEPRESS PUBLISHING

© 2007 by Kathy Kirk. All rights reserved.

Pleasant Word (a division of WinePress Publishing, PO Box 428, Enumclaw, WA 98022) functions only as book publisher. As such, the ultimate design, content, editorial accuracy, and views expressed or implied in this work are those of the author.

No part of this publication may be reproduced, stored in a retrieval system or transmitted in any way by any means—electronic, mechanical, photocopy, recording or otherwise—without the prior permission of the copyright holder, except as provided by USA copyright law.

Content, Design, Photography, and/or Cover may not be reproduced in whole or in part in any form without the express written consent of Kathy Kirk.

Unless otherwise indicated, all Scriptures are taken from the New American Standard Bible® (NASB®) Copyright © The Lockman Foundation 1960, 1962, 1963, 1968, 1971, 1972, 1973, 1975, 1977, 1995. Used by permission.

Permission to quote from the following additional copyrighted versions of the Bible is acknowledged with appreciation:

Scripture references marked NLT are taken from New Living Translation. Copyright © Tyndale House Publishers, Inc., Wheaton, IL 60189. All rights reserved.

Scripture references marked NIV are taken from the Holy Bible, New International Version, Copyright © 1973, 1978, 1984 by the International Bible Society. Used by permission of Zondervan Publishing House. The "NIV" and "New International Version" trademarks are registered in the United States Patent and Trademark Office by International Bible Society.

Scripture references marked TM are taken from The Message Bible © 1993 by Eugene N. Peterson, NavPress, POB 35001, Colorado Springs, CO 80935, 4th printing in USA 1994. Published in association with the literary agency—Aline Comm. POB 49068, Colorado Springs, CO 80949. Used by permission.

Scripture references marked CEV are taken from Contemporary English Version. Copyright © by American Bible Society, 1991, 1992. Used by permission. All rights reserved.

Photography on pages 16, 23, 40, 138 by BigStockPhoto (c) 2004-2006. All rights reserved.
All Other Photography: Lisa Landrum.
Italics in scripture quotations were added by author for emphasis.

ISBN 13: 978-1-4141-0853-7
ISBN 10: 1-4141-0853-2
Library of Congress Catalog Card Number: 2006908388

Table of Contents

Acknowledgements vii
A Message to Parents.. ix
How to Use this Book.. xi
Introduction xv

PART I: I BELONG TO GOD

Chapter 1: God Created the Earth 21
Chapter 2: God Created Me 27
Chapter 3: God Made Me Special... 31
Chapter 4 : We Belong to God.. 35
Chapter 5: Who is God?.. 39
Chapter 6 : God Wants the Best for Us.................................... 45

PART II: MY NEED FOR SALVATION

Chapter 7 : The First Sin 55
Chapter 8 : God Allows Us to Make Choices 59
Chapter 9 : Bad Behavior Must be Disciplined 63
Chapter 10: Why Do We Need to Be Saved? 67
Chapter 11: Benefits to Being Saved.. 71

Part III: My Salvation

Chapter 12: Jesus Is Our Superhero 81
Chapter 13: Children Need To Be Saved 85
Chapter 14: What If I Sin After I am Saved? 89
Chapter 15: Believe that Jesus is Lord 93
Chapter 16: Tell God What You Have Done 97
Chapter 17: Do Things God's Way 101
Chapter 18: Just Say These Words 105

Part IV: My Life After I Am Saved

Chapter 19: Jesus Can Help Me Stop Doing Bad Things 117
Chapter 20: Love Gifts from Jesus 121
Chapter 21: What Do I Do After I Sin? 125
Chapter 22: How Does God Forgive? 129
Chapter 23: Find a Christian Mentor and
   Christian Friends 133
Chapter 24: Myths About Being Saved 137

Part V: My Challenges as a Christian

Chapter 25: I'm Saved, but I Keep Sinning 145
Chapter 26: The Tricks of the Devil 149
Chapter 27: We Are Selfish 153
Chapter 28: God Gives Us Tests Too 157
Chapter 29: Why Do Bad Things Happen to Christians? 161
Chapter 30: Choose Today Whom You Will Serve 165

Answer Key 175

Acknowledgements

My thanks to God who poured into me the content for this series of books and for using me as a vessel. I want to thank my husband, Gerald, and my children, Maya and Cameron, for being patient with me during the writing. Thanks to all of my dear family and friends who did not abandon me even though I abandoned them during this writing. Special thanks to Janice White, Kristen Davis and Freda Dents who read and reread my copy and solicited valuable comments.

A Message to Parents

This book is designed to encourage parents and children to study the Word of God together. So many times parents go to Bible studies, read the Bible, or talk to Christian friends to learn more about God and leave their children's growth up to the church. The church only gets a few hours on the weekend to share the gospel with your child. What are your children getting the other six days of the week?

As parents, our main job is to minister to our families. What better person to share the gospel with your children than you? If you do not lead your children to Christ, someone else will lead him or her away from Christ. As Dr. Randy Carlson, a Christian psychologist, says, "We need to be intentional parents."

Intentional parents are those who are taking the lead in their children's spiritual development. It is never too early to teach your children about God. The best way to teach your children is to lead by example.

In our world today, the lines are blurred between Christians and non-Christians. No one knows who is or isn't a Christian, because the majority of Christians look just like the world. Romans 12:2 (NLT) tells us, "*Do not copy the behaviors and customs of this world, but let God transform you into a new person by changing the way you think.*" It is important that parents paint the correct picture of what God expects from us and not the watered-down version. God will reward parents on their ability to raised godly children.

To raise godly children, you must act godly as well. Your children will imitate your behavior whether it is good or bad. They will learn what it means to be a Christian by what you do, if you claim to be saved. Will your behavior cause them to sin or obey God? Matthew 18:6 (NIV) tells us, *"But if anyone causes one of these little ones who believe in me to sin, it would be better for him to have a large millstone hung around his neck and to be drowned in the depths of the sea."* What are you doing or not doing that will cause your children to sin? Are you going to church regularly, forgiving others, exhibiting the fruit of the spirit, using wholesome words, and obeying God completely?

These books are designed to help parents, as well as children, grow. My children have asked many questions during this study, so I have put on my website answers to their questions and many others. Visit www.mychildsheart.org to find answers to some of your questions. I pray that the series of *My Child's Heart* will be a blessing for you and your family.

How to Use this Book

This book will help parents and children understand what it means to be saved. I want to encourage you to set aside time daily to read this book. God tells us that we should meditate on His Word day and night. What better way to start your day? You can set aside 15 minutes in the morning to take turns reading or read it at the table during family dinner. My family takes turns reading each paragraph and answering the questions at dinner time, and this has been a lot of fun. You can also add this to your bedtime routine. It doesn't matter when you do it–just do it.

This book is divided into five sections. Each section has five to seven short devotionals. Read one devotional daily. At the end of each devotional, answer the **Think About It** questions. They will help you think about what you have read and how it fits into your life. The parent questions are designed to demonstrate to your children that you had and have similar experiences and challenges. Please be mindful of your children's ages, and share only age-appropriate things. This is not the time to air all your dirty laundry. A **Key Verse** has been listed to help you remember what you have read. The **Key Verse** will help you obey God, remember how awesome God is, or help you not to be afraid. **Prayer Time** is the time set aside for you to talk to God. Each devotional has a short prayer about what you have read. Please feel free to add more to this prayer. This is a time for you to share everything with God.

Once you get to the end of a section, there is a page called **Play It Again**. It is a review of the things you have already read. This section is fun because you will have games to play to help you remember what you have read.

Parent and child can challenge each other in the Bible Quiz section to see who knows the most. Read your sections every day so you will be able to do the fun sections together. The **Play It Again** sections can be used as your weekend devotion.

I have found that it is easier to stay focused on God when you surround yourself with those who will hold you accountable. This book is great for book clubs, Sunday school, and classrooms. Start a book club with other children and parents and meet once a week or after the completion of the book to discuss the material. My website www.mychildsheart.org, has group discussion questions and fun activities for each book. Allow at least two hours to fully answer the questions and to allow the children time to mingle and

How to Use this Book

share their experiences with God. A small group will help you and your children establish relationships with those who are trying to please God.

It is easier for children to follow Christ when they know they are not alone. You want to establish a long-term relationship with those who are seeking God seriously. To continue developing devoted Christians, I am completing a series of books that can be read by your book club. Look for the following exciting topics in the *My Child's Heart* book series.

Salvation Starts In The Heart
What Goes In Must Come Out
My Friends And Siblings Are Driving Me Crazy
I Don't Like Being Told What To Do
The World Looks Good To Me

Introduction

Do you have questions about what it means to be saved and what you are being saved from? Being saved is just another way of saying that you are a Christian. Do you know what it really means to be a Christian? You are probably thinking *I know what a Christian is*, but do you really? I ask this question because I thought I was saved at the age of six and didn't realize that I wasn't until my twenties. How dumb was that? Not dumb at all, because no one ever explained to me what it means to be saved. I thought believing in Jesus Christ and going to church made me saved. I realized as I got older that it is much more than that.

So what does a Christian look and act like? Are the people sitting on the pews at church Christians, are your friends who are unkind to you Christians? What about people who are kind to you but never say anything about Jesus Christ? Well, in this book we will answer these questions and many more like:

- Can I wait until I am older to be saved?
- Can I get to heaven by just doing good things?
- Am I saved even though I sin?
- When I'm saved can I just keep on sinning and just ask for forgiveness?

My Child's Heart

- Does everybody sin?
- Can other religions get me to heaven?
- Are children automatically saved?

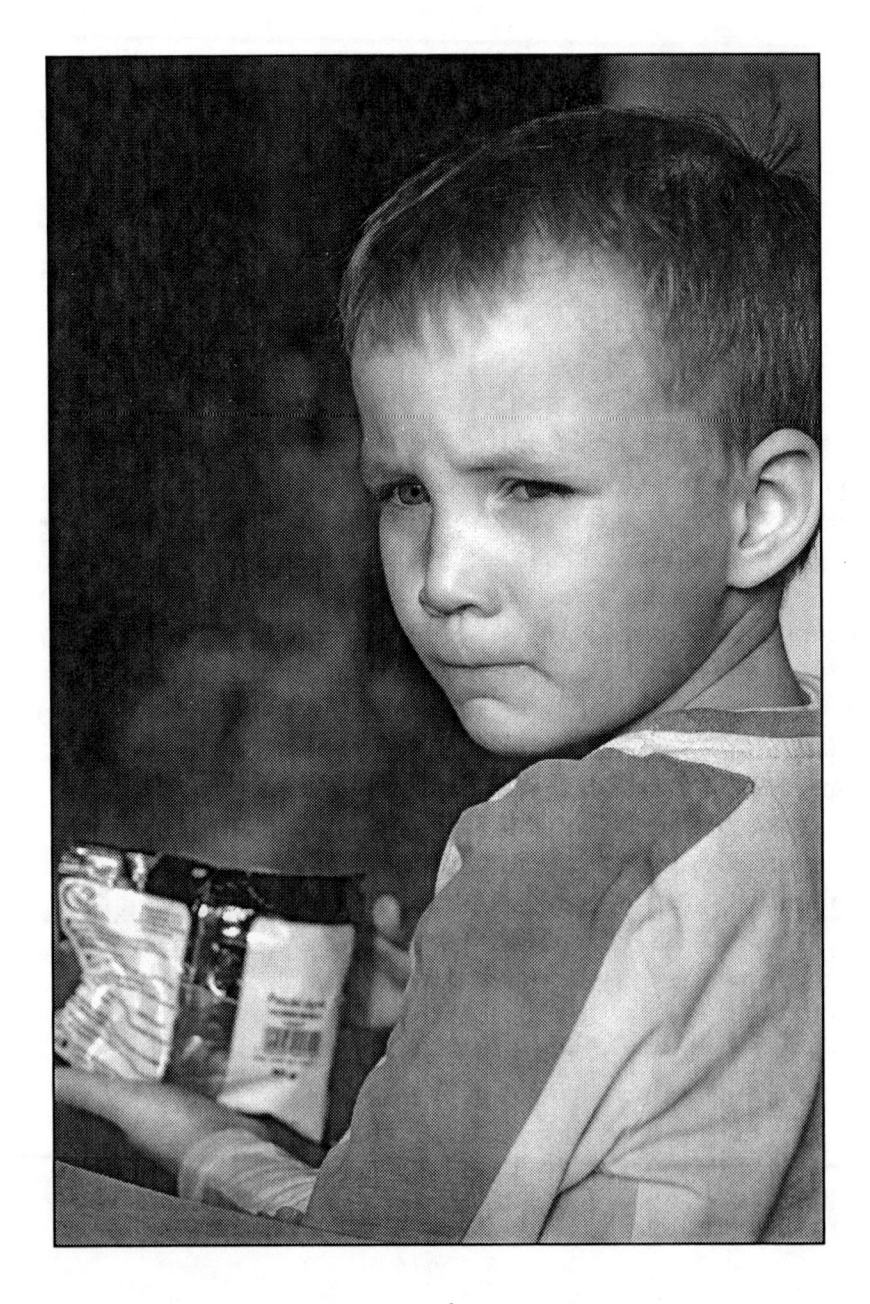

Introduction

To answer these questions, we will start with the beginning. Some of you are probably thinking the beginning of what? We will start with the beginning of the Bible. By starting here, we will better understand our need to be saved. The Bible is one of the most important books you can read. It can be such an awesome read if you have the right Bible. The New International Version (NIV) is great for young readers. In fact, there are Bibles just for young readers like you. Go to a Christian bookstore, check them out, and get the one right for you.

As we journey through the Bible, we will read exciting stories about people who pleased God and those who were not able to please God. These people are just like you and me. Did you know there are heroes and villains in the Bible? Well, we will talk about the hero and the villain of the Bible as well.

Most importantly, we will read about how God loves us and accepts us for who we are.

Each book of the Bible was written by someone, but God told him what to say. I have written the Bible verses directly from the Bible so you can follow along easily and so you can get used to reading the Bible. I have italicized for you every word that is from the Bible. God uses the Bible to teach us everything we need to know about pleasing Him. It is going to be a fun adventure, so pay close attention to see what you can learn by just reading the Bible.

The book of Genesis was written by Moses. So open up your Bibles to Gen. 1:1, and let's see what Moses has to say about creation.

PART 1
I Belong to God

Chapter 1
God Created the Earth

This story begins when only God existed—God the Father, Son, and Holy Spirit. *"In the beginning God created the heavens and the earth. The earth was barren, with no form of life; it was under a roaring ocean covered with darkness"* (Gen. 1:1, CEV). There was nothing—no houses, no land, no trees, no people. Everything was covered by water. *"But the Spirit of God was moving over the water"* (Gen. 1:2, CEV).

> *"God said, 'I command light to shine!' And light started shining. He separated light from darkness and named the light 'Day' and the darkness 'Night.' Evening came and then morning—that was the first day."*
>
> (Gen. 1:3-5 CEV)

"God said, 'I command a dome to separate the water above it from the water below it.' God said, 'I command the water under the sky to come together in one place, so there will be dry ground.' God named the dry ground 'Land,' and he named the water 'Ocean'" (Gen. 1:6-10, CEV). Where do you live in this wonderful world that God created? What is the best thing about where you live?

"God said, 'I command the earth to produce all kinds of plants, including fruit trees and grain'" (Gen. 1:11, CEV). The earth is able to produce all the wonderful things that we eat each day like corn, broccoli, greens, and zucchini. God made all of these great vegetables to keep us healthy.

Did You Know?

Doctors say that we should eat vegetables and fruit to stay healthy. We need the vitamins and fibers from these foods.

Eat 4 servings of vegetables everyday, such as carrots, broccoli, green beans, peas, lettuce, celery, others.

Eat 4 servings of fruit everyday, such as apples, oranges, bananas, pineapples, peaches, melons, grapes, others.

Vegetables and fruits are needed because they:

- Keep our teeth and gums healthy
- Keep our skin and hair healthy
- Help with growth and eyesight
- Help us work our muscles
- Give us energy
- Help our hearts stay healthy

Are you eating at least four vegetables and four fruits a day? By eating a vegetable and fruit with every meal, you will almost get what you need to stay healthy. Eating healthy is important for Christians, because we need to keep our bodies healthy so we will have the energy and strength to share the good news about Jesus.

God didn't stop here so let's go on. *"God said, 'I command lights to appear in the sky and to separate day from night and to show the time for seasons, special days, and years'"* (Gen. 1:14, CEV).

God Created the Earth

So now we have all of our wonderful seasons like winter, spring, summer, and fall. I like all of these seasons except winter. Where I live it gets very cold and snows in the wintertime. My children love it, because they get to play in the snow and throw snowballs at my husband and me.

"God made two powerful lights, the brighter one to rule the day and the other to rule the night. He also made the stars" (Gen. 1:16, CEV). Although God made the stars, we should not use the stars (horoscope) to tell the future. Some people do this, so be aware that God tells us not to do this in Deuteronomy 18:1-12. *"Then God put these lights in the sky to shine on the earth, to rule day and night, and to separate light from darkness"* (Gen. 1:17-18, CEV). Now

we have stars, a moon, and sun. Isn't this interesting, hearing how the world came together?

Did You Know?

    The sun is 100 times larger than the earth. It's the center of our solar system, and without it our planet would be just a hard, cold rock. No people, plants, or animals could live here. Everything needs the warmth and light of the sun to live. But too much sun can be bad for us too.

God Created the Earth

Think About It

Parent/Teacher:

- Tell your children about a time God provided for you.
- Discuss your current eating habits and what the family could do to eat healthier.

Children:

- What did you learn about God?
- List how you are going to eat the needed vegetables and fruits every day.
- What vegetables and fruits would you like for your parents to buy?
- Did you learn anything new?

Key Verse

In the beginning God made heaven and earth.

(Gen. 1:1, CEV)

Prayer Time

Dear God, thank you for making such a wonderful place for me to live. Help me enjoy all of your creations. Please help me eat right. Amen.

Chapter 2
God Created Me

God said, 'I command the ocean to be full of living creatures, and I command birds to fly above the earth'" (Gen. 1:20, CEV). Isn't God wonderful? He gave us birds and all of the wonderful seafood I love to eat. I love birds; we have a cockatiel name "Elmo". Cockatiels are great, because they can learn to talk.

> "God said, 'I command the earth to give life to all kinds of tame animals, wild animals, and reptiles.'"
>
> "God said, 'Now we will make humans, and they will be like us. We will let them rule the fish, the birds, and all other living creatures'"
>
> (Gen. 1:24,26, CEV)

"God said, 'Now we will make humans and they will be like us'"(Gen. 1:26, CEV). Who do you think God was talking to when He said, "We" above? He was talking to Jesus. *"In the beginning was the Word and the Word was with God, and the Word was God"* (John 1:1, NIV). The "Word" is a special name for Jesus. So the Bible tells us that Jesus was there in the beginning with God and became human like us later on to save us. So God created humans to be like himself; He made men and women.

Wow, God made all of these wonderful things just by saying it. Isn't God awesome and powerful? Everything that is on this earth was made by God. God was here before the world was formed, and He made everything. No matter what anyone else says, believe that God made everything. It may sound confusing, and others may tell you stories of how they think the world came into existence, but remember, God made it all. You may not be able to explain how He did it, and that is okay. Just believe that He did!

God Created Me

Think About It

Parent/Teacher:

- Discuss the meaning of these four characteristics of Jesus with your children: faithful, forgiving, loving, unselfish.
- Explain to your children how you use these characteristics every day in your personal life.

Children:

- How can you use the characteristics of Jesus that we discussed above?
- What did you learn about God?
- List two ways you can behave that would show people that you were made like God.

Key Verse

The Spirit of God has made me; the breath of the Almighty gives me life.

(Job 33:4, NIV)

Prayer Time

Dear God, help me remember that you created everything, including me. Please help me show my love for you every day. Amen.

Chapter 3
God Made Me Special

God created everything, and that includes you and me. Psalm 24:1 (NIV) tells us that, "*The earth is the LORD's, and everything in it, the world, and all who live in it*". Everything you see around you, God created. The things you see in nature did not just happen. The people you see around you did not just happen.

1. Genesis tells us that God created everything. Go outside and write down some of the wonderful things you can see that God made.

    1. _____
    2. _____
    3. _____

2. Look at 3 different animals and write down how they are different from each other.

    1. _____
    2. _____
    3. _____

My Child's Heart

Did you notice how different all of the creatures are? God made all of us different. Since God makes everything, He made you and me. You are as beautiful as the world outside. He made us all different–just like the animals you saw outside are different. Do you look exactly like your sibling? I have two children, and their skin and eye colors are different from one another. I love my children even though they look different. God loves all of us, because we are His children. Just think how boring it would be eating ice cream if we had only vanilla. Just like God gave us variety in ice cream, He has given us variety in people. Although we are different, we are all very special to God.

Maybe you think you are too tall or too short. Maybe you think you are too skinny or too fat; or your hair is too short or too long. You may even think your skin color is all wrong. Remember, God made you exactly how He wants you to be. You may not look like your friends, and that is okay. It is important that you love how God made you. What God thinks about you should matter more than what anyone else thinks. You don't have to be perfect to have God's love.

Stephanie was so bummed because she was taller than her friends—even the boys. She got teased a lot because of her height. She couldn't understand why God would make her so different from all of her friends. Because of her long legs and skinny body, it was hard for her parents to find clothing to fit her. Her mother had to make most of her clothing. This was a drag, because she couldn't wear clothes that looked like what her friends wore. This made her feel unhappy, and she felt this way for a long time. When she went to middle school, someone told her that she should try out for the track team. She tried out and found out that she could run faster than most of the girls. This made her feel good. She was so fast that she came in first place in most of the track meets. She couldn't believe that God had given her these wonderful long legs to run. She no longer felt bad about being tall but felt glad that God had made her so special.

Stephanie thought that God had made her different but later realized that God had made her special. He made you special as well!

God Made Me Special

Maya, saved at age 9. She said,
"I feel good about being saved."

Joke Time
Knock, knock!
Who's there?
Psalm.
Psalm, who?
Psalmbody important!

THINK ABOUT IT

Parent/Teacher:

- Discuss two physical things that you like and dislike about yourself.
- How does it make you feel to know that God knows everything about you?
- Write down 5 things that are special about each child on a separate sheet of paper. Read these aloud, and give the paper to the child to keep.

Children:

- Discuss two physical things that you like and dislike about yourself.
- Did you learn anything new?

Key Verse

I've loved you the way my Father has loved Me.
                                                    (John 15:9a, TM)

Prayer Time

Dear God, thank you for making me the way I am. Help me with the things I dislike about myself. Amen.

Chapter 4
We Belong to God

Because God created the first person, He has the right to tell all of us what to do. Every person alive is under God's command. Let's say that your family goes to the pet store and purchases a puppy. Once you purchase the puppy, you own it. You get to decide what to call the puppy. You decide where the puppy will sleep and what the puppy will eat. Your family has complete control over this puppy.

You teach the puppy what is right and wrong. You discipline the puppy when he doesn't do what you tell him to do.

We are kind of like this puppy. God created us, so He owns us. He tells us what He expects from us in the Bible. This is exactly what He did with Adam and Eve. He told them what He expected from them. When we do what God tells us to do, He is pleased with us. When we disobey God, He is unhappy with us. God is so awesome, because He still loves us, even when we disobey Him.

We Belong to God

Think About It

Parent/Teacher:

- Does God own you?
- Who else has a right to tell you what to do?

Children:

- What did you learn about God?
- Since God owns you, do you have to do what He says?
- Where does God tell us what He wants us to do?

Key Verse

The earth is the Lord's, and everything in it, the world, and all who live in it.

(Ps. 24:1, NIV)

Prayer Time

Dear God, please help me to obey your commands. I thank you that you made me special. Please help me to love the way you made me and love others for the way you made them. Amen.

Chapter 5
Who is God?

We learned that God is the creator of everything and that He is real in Gen. 1:1. What else do we know about God? To find out about God, we have to go to the Bible. The Bible tells us everything that God wants us to know about Him. So let's look at Scripture to see what we can find out.

1. God is ruler of heaven and earth. There's no other God.

"Know therefore today, and take it to your heart, that the Lord, He is God in heaven above and on the earth below; there is no other."
(Deut. 4:39, NASB)

2. God is righteous.

"The Lord is righteous in all His ways and loving toward all He has made."
(Ps. 145:17, NIV)

Isaiah tells us that God is righteous. Righteous means without sin. We also learn that God loves everything that He has made. And since He made you, God loves you.

3. God is everywhere.

"You know when I sit and when I rise; You perceive my thoughts from afar. You discern my going out and my lying down; You are familiar with all my ways."

(Ps. 139:2-3, NIV)

How can God know what we are doing all of the time? How can He be with me and with you all the time? The Bible tells us that God is everywhere. When your parents can't be with you, God can.

Who is God?

4. God knows everything.

"Great is our Lord and mighty in power; His understanding has no limit."

(Ps. 147:5, NIV)

God knows everything and can do anything. We saw the awesome power of God when He created the world.

God can create the world and help you deal with your problems too.

5. God is made up of three equal persons.

"May the grace of the Lord Jesus Christ and the love of God and the fellowship of the Holy Spirit be with you all."

(2 Cor. 13:14, NIV)

The Bible tells us there is only one God but that God is three equal persons. This is called the Trinity (God the Father, God the Son, and God the Holy Spirit). Trinity means three in one.

6. God loves all of us, even while we are sinners.

"For God so loved the world that He gave His one and only Son that whoever believes in Him shall not perish but have everlasting life."

(John 3:16, NIV)

God loves us dearly. He wants to be our friend. Because Adam and Eve sinned, God had to make plans for us to come to Him and that was done by the death of Jesus Christ.

7. God is invisible but revealed to us through Jesus.

"No one has ever seen God. The only Son, who is truly God and is closest to the Father, has shown us what God is like."

(John 1:18, CEV)

Wow, no one has seen God. Jesus came on earth so that we will know what God is like. By looking at Jesus, we can see God.

Did You Know?

You are made up of more than 50% water. Your blood is made up mostly of water. Water helps move nutrients to your organs and removes waste material from your body.

Who is God?

THINK ABOUT IT

Parent/Teacher:

- Share about a time when you where all alone and frightened, but God helped you make it through.
- Tell about something God has given you for which you are thankful.

Children:

- What did you learn about God?
- Are you sometimes afraid to sleep in your room alone or afraid of someone or something? Who did you find out is always with you?
- How should you act if God is always with you?

Key Verse

For God so loved the world that He gave His one and only Son that whoever believes in Him shall not perish but have everlasting life.
(John 3:16, NIV)

Prayer Time

Dear God, help me to understand fully the love you have for me. Help me to know that you are powerful and can do anything. Amen.

Chapter 6
God Wants the Best for Us

"The Lord made a garden in a place called Eden, which was in the east, and he put the man there. The Lord God placed all kinds of beautiful trees and fruit trees in the garden. Two other trees were in the middle of the garden. One of the trees gave life–the other gave the power to know the difference between right and wrong. The Lord God put the man in the Garden of Eden to take care of it and to look after it. But the Lord told him, 'You may eat fruit from any tree in the garden, except the one that has the power to let you know the difference between right and wrong. If you eat any fruit from that tree, you will die before the day is over!'"

(Gen. 2:8-17, CEV)

God gave Adam and Eve rules to protect them. Your parents give you rules to protect you. He told them that they would die if they ate from the forbidden tree. Most of you probably know that they didn't die. So what does the word "die" mean? Die means to be separated from God. They would not have a relationship with God. Since God owns us, He has the right to set the rules and the consequences for breaking the rules. God makes rules because He loves us and wants to protect us.

Since God wants the best for us, He has given people authority over us. Hebrews 13:17 (NIV) says, *"Obey your leaders and submit to their authority. They keep watch over you as men who must give an account. Obey them so that their work will be a joy, not a burden, for that would be of no advantage to you."*

God is telling us that He expects us to obey those in authority. Authority means the right to tell you what to do. Your parents, teachers, and pastor are a few people who have authority over you. All people have someone of authority over them. Being under authority is not a bad thing. In fact, God says if you submit to those in authority, things will go well for you.

God has given your parents complete authority over you. Their job is to help you be obedient to God.

Proverbs 19:18 (NLT) says, *"Discipline your children while there is hope. If you don't, you will ruin their lives."* It is important for your parents to discipline you when you do wrong. Discipline helps change your bad behavior to good behavior.

The Ten Commandments tell us to honor our parents, so our lives will be long. By doing what your parents tell you to do, you will have a better life. God will bless you.

God Wants the Best for Us

When you learn to be obedient to your parents without arguing, whining, and talking back, you are closer to being able to be obedient to God's commands. There are so many people in this world who have no one to show them the ways of God. They face many problems and miss out on many blessings. Having godly parents and others around you who are concerned about what you do is a blessing.

Think About It

Parent/Teacher:

- Discuss two rules that you must follow and the consequences of breaking them.
- Discuss two rules that you have for your children and how these rules will protect them.

Children:

- Why did God make rules for us?
- Why is it important to be obedient to your parents?
- Did you learn anything new?

Key Verse

Listen to my instruction and be wise.
(Prov. 8:33a, NIV)

Prayer Time

Dear God, thank you for loving me enough to provide commands that will make my life easier. Help me to be obedient to my parents and your commands. Amen.

God Wants the Best for Us

Play It Again #1

Do you remember what you read? Answer the questions below to see how much you know.

1. Who made everything?

2. Was Jesus with God in the beginning?

   _____ a. Yes _____ b. No

3. How shall I act toward God, since He owns me?

   _____ a. Do whatever I want to do.
   _____ b. Do what my friends are doing.
   _____ c. Do what God tells me to do in the Bible.
   _____ d. Do what is fun.

4. Does God have a right to expect me to do what He tells me to do?

   _____ a. Yes _____ b. No

5. What is God's role as owner?

   _____ a. To be our buddy.
   _____ b. To set rules and correct us when we are wrong.
   _____ c. To ignore our bad behavior.

5. Who are the three persons of the Trinity?

BIBLE QUIZ #1

(Challenge your parents and see what they know.)

1. Write the day (1-7) in-which God made the following (Gen. 1:5-24).

    _____ Rested

    _____ Separated the water and sky

    _____ Sun, moon, stars

    _____ Animals and man

    _____ Day and night

    _____ Dry land, grass, and trees

    _____ Whales, creatures in the sea, creatures in the air

2. In what battle did the sun stand still (Josh. 10:12)?

    _____ a. Gideon

    _____ b. Jericho

    _____ c. Moabites

3. Eve was made first (Gen. 2:21-22).

    _____ a. True   _____ b. False

4. Was the Holy Spirit with God in the beginning (Gen. 1:1)?

    _____ a. Yes   _____ b. No

God Wants the Best for Us

Fun Time #1

Unscramble these names in the Bible

HNOA   _____

JPSOEH   _____

MDAA   _____

VDIAD   _____

THSE   _____

WMTTAHE   _____

CBJOA   _____

My Child's Heart

Fun Time # 1

Find the hidden words

```
S O M J W S E S P E C I A L W
Q E T D P C V G G E G S U T I
L V L I H B E N L S G L O R O
E Z R B C S U O Y W M M A I Y
B I K Z A D H L T O N C Y T P
T A E I R T Z E F Y J B I K S
X C R L I Z E B L G W N P Y V
Y K U R R L V G U H I D A L C
G H W H E O K O E R T S F A R
S O A K G N V J T V M R R Q E
U R D L L X Q U D T M E A S A
S A D A M D L R O W H S R E T
E R E H W Y R E V E O A K R E
J N L A A C C Z T C T N P K G
J R R E B I Y G J S Z P T U F
```

ADAM   EVE   SPIRIT
BARREN   EVERYWHERE   STARS
BELONGS   GOD   TRINITY
CREATE   JESUS   VEGETABLES
EARTH   SPECIAL   WORLD

Part II
My Need for Salvation

Chapter 7
The First Sin

> "When the Woman saw that the tree looked like good eating and realized what she would get out of it—she'd know everything!—she took and ate the fruit and then gave some to her husband, and he ate. ...So G<small>OD</small> expelled them from the Garden of Eden and sent them to work the ground, the same dirt out of which they'd been made. He threw them out of the garden and stationed angel-cherubim and a revolving sword of fire east of it, guarding the path to the Tree-of-Life."
>
> (Gen. 3:6, 23-24, T<small>M</small>)

Adam and Eve ate the fruit from the tree that God told them not to eat from. They disobeyed God's command, which is a sin.

Sin—not doing what God tells us to do

Have your parents ever told you not to eat candy or sweets before dinner? You probably didn't understand why you couldn't eat the candy. In fact, you probably thought it was silly. Hopefully, you obeyed them. If you didn't obey, you sinned. You will not always understand or agree with God's rules or your parent's rules, but you must obey them.

God tells children to obey their parents, and when you do not, that is sin.

Let's take a look at why Eve sinned. Eve was talked into sinning by someone else. Satan told her that God was telling a lie about the tree, and she believed him over God. It is important for you to know what God says in the Bible. You also have to believe the things that God says in the Bible, because Satan will try to trick you.

Satan will tell you that it is okay to hang around kids who do bad things and that you are saved, so they can't convince you to do bad things. Some of this is true, because you are saved, but the Bible tells us, *"bad company corrupts good morals"* (1 Cor. 15:33, NASB). He might tell you that it is okay to sin, because God is a forgiving God. He is correct when he says, "God is a forgiving God." But if sin is okay, the Bible wouldn't tell us in Romans 6:23 that the wages of sin is death.

Eve also thought it would be good to know everything that God knows. Have you ever wanted something so badly that you

The First Sin

were willing to steal it? So many times we sin because of something we see and want badly. Most things don't become attractive to us until our friends get it. When our friends get it, we feel like we must have it. This is what happened to Eve. Eve wanted to be smart like God.

Eve ate the fruit, and then gave it to Adam. Adam knew that God told them not to eat the fruit. He ate it, probably, because he didn't want Eve to be the only smart one. He didn't want to miss out on the fun. This is what we call *peer pressure*. Have you ever had a friend talk you into doing something bad? Have you ever done something unkind to others to make your friends laugh? If you have to do bad things or unkind things to others to make friends, you don't want these people as friends. Friends should help you do the right thing.

Think About It

Parent/Teacher:

- Discuss a time when a friend talked you into doing something bad. What was the consequence?
- Share with your children how important it is to choose godly friends.

Children:

- What did you learn about God?
- What should Adam have told Eve when she asked him to eat the fruit?
- List all of your close friends. Next to their names write whether they try to help you do the right thing or wrong thing most of the time.

Key Verse

I have hidden your word in my heart that I might not sin against you.
(Ps 119:11, NIV)

Prayer Time

Dear God, help me to study your word daily to keep me from sinning against you. Please help me choose friends that will help me do the right thing. Amen.

Chapter 8
God Allows Us to Make Choices

Since God created us, He loves us and knows what is best for us. God showed His love for Adam and Eve by giving them all they needed–food and a place to live. He also gave Adam and Eve boundaries to protect them. Things would go well for them as long as they did what He said.

God has given us each the ability to make choices. God does not force us to do things His way. If He did, we would be like robots. Can you image all of us walking around doing and saying the same thing? God tests us to see if we are going to choose the right way.

Did Adam and Eve make a good choice by eating the fruit?

Adam and Eve disobeyed God when they ate the fruit from the forbidden tree. They committed the first sin. Have you ever sinned? The answer to this question should be yes, because God tells us that we are all sinners. *"There's nobody living right, not even one"* (Rom. 3:10, TM). And since we are all sinners, we need to be saved. You may be thinking, *What have I done that is a sin?* A sin is not doing what God tells us in the Bible we should do.

COMMON SINS

Lying	Stealing
Cheating	Disobeying parents/teachers
Fighting	Talking bad about someone
Selfishness	Not forgiving
Complaining	Not listening to God

What we *think* can also be a sin. God knows everything that we are thinking. You can sin just by thinking bad thoughts. So if you are thinking that you hate someone or wish something bad would happen to someone, that is a sin.

You also sin when you wish for someone to lose at a game.

When we sin, we push God away from us. The more we sin, the further He moves away from us. When we do what God tells us to do, He is like our shadow. When we sin a little, He is like our next door neighbor. When we sin a lot, it is like He is in another state. Have you ever driven out of the state for vacation or to visit relatives? It normally takes hours to get there. Wouldn't it be nicer to have God right next to you instead of in another state?

God Allows Us to Make Choices

Remember, God loves you no matter how much you sin. You may sin a lot, but God is excited to see you, just like your relatives are who live in a different state. You may push God away because of your sins, but His arms are long enough to hug you no matter where you are. He will always love you and forgive your sins.

Did You Know?

There are consequences to our sins. Blessings come from doing right. When we do wrong, we have bad consequences. Let's take a look at the Bible to see some of the consequences of not doing what God tells us to do.

Action	Consequence
Disobey parents	**Will have a shortened life.** "Children, obey your parents in the Lord, for this is right. "That it may go well with you and that you may enjoy long life on the earth." (Eph. 6:1,3, NIV)
Lie	**Parent will not trust you and you will be punished.** "Dishonest witnesses and liars won't escape punishment." (Prov. 19:5, CEV)
Don't take care of clothing, toys, and other things that people give you.	**Will not get the things you want from parents and God.** "And if you have not been trustworthy with someone else's property, who will give you property of your own?" (Luke 16:12, NIV)

Think About It

Parent/Teacher:

- Share two of your current sins. Make sure that your discussion is child friendly and appropriate. Use the concordance in your Bible to locate scripture that will help you with your sins. Write the scriptures down and say them everyday.
- Share something you do that pleases God.

Children:

- Share two of your current sins. Use the concordance in your Bible to locate scripture that will help you with your sins. Write the scriptures down and say them everyday.
- What does God do to us when we sin?
- Share something that you do that pleases God.

Key Verse

The fear of the LORD is the beginning of wisdom; all who follow his precepts have good understanding.

(Ps. 111:10, NIV)

Prayer Time

Dear God, please help me hear and obey your word. I know by listening to you, I will make wise choices. Amen.

Chapter 9
Bad Behavior Must be Disciplined

God tells us what to do in the Bible. We get out of God's circle of protection when we sin. When we are out of His circle of protection, bad things happen to us. When you cross the street, there are normally lines and light signals to direct you across the street safely. When you cross the street outside the lines or on a red light, you might get hit by a car. These street-crossing rules are necessary to protect you; just like God's rules in the Bible are there to protect you.

Adam and Eve's circle of protection was in the Garden of Eden. God kicked them out of the garden, and life was hard for them after that.

I bet some of you are saying, "This is harsh punishment for just eating the fruit." Well, God expects us to do everything He tells us to do. We cannot pick and choose what we will and will not do. God will discipline us when we disobey Him. *Discipline* means to teach or instruct. Discipline causes us to change our behavior.

Don't look at this as God being mean. Look at Him in the same way you look at your parents. Proverbs 16:6b (NASB) tells us, *"And by the fear of the Lord one keeps away from evil."* This fear means to honor, respect, and love.

My Child's Heart

I feared my mother, because I knew she would discipline me when I did wrong. She did this out of love for me. The best thing about this fear is that it prevented me from doing the wrong thing. My mother tells me that I was a very good child. She had no problems with me. Some of my siblings stayed in trouble and were frequently punished. I was not frequently punished, because I did what my mother told me to do. This is exactly how God is. Bad consequences and punishments help us change our ways. Without them, we would continue to sin and have a terrible life. I am glad my mother showed me the importance of submitting to authority. This made it easier for me to understand, love, and submit to God.

Sarah had a hard time keeping her room clean, and her parents kept begging her to clean her room.

Every day they walked by and shook their heads at how messy her room was. When they told her to clean her room, she would. But the next day, her room was a mess again. Her parents couldn't understand why she couldn't keep her room clean. They became

Bad Behavior Must be Disciplined

very frustrated with her. They decided to talk to one of their friends about this problem. Their friend asked if they had punished her for this bad behavior. Her parents realized that they had not. So they decided to take away her television for a week. She kept her room clean for a few days, and then it was back to being messy again. Her parents had to punish her time after time until she got tired of missing out on her favorite television shows.

Do you think Sarah would have stopped if her parents hadn't punished her? Sarah was not honoring her parents when she kept her room messy. It was important that her parents teach her to be obedient to them. Punishments help us do the right thing. God was sad about having to kick Adam and Eve out of the Garden of Eden. He wanted them to be a part of His family forever.

Think About It

Parent/Teacher:

- Share a time when you did something bad, and there was a bad consequence or punishment.
- Read Deut. 5:21 about coveting, which means to want badly or crave, and tell how this commandment can protect you.
- Read 1 Cor. 6:10 to find out the punishment for being covetous.

Children:

- What did you learn about God?
- Share a time when you did something bad, and there was a bad consequence or punishment.
- List some actions that would take you out of God's circle of safety.

Key Verse

Do not withhold your mercy from me, O Lord; may your love and your truth always protect me.

(Ps. 40:11, NIV)

Prayer Time

Dear God, I want to be protected by you. Please help me be obedient so I can stay in your circle of protection. Amen.

Chapter 10
Why Do We Need to Be Saved?

We have to be saved, because Adam and Eve sinned. The Bible tells us that we all have been born sinners and need to be saved. God designed us to have a relationship with Him. That relationship was broken when Adam and Eve sinned. Because of our sin, we are not fit to join God in heaven.

Write down the name of a friend that you have chosen to have a relationship with. _____

Did that friend *make* you be his or her friend? _____

It is probably safe to say that you chose to be that person's friend. Well, we must *choose* to be friends with God as well.

John and his family decided to go out to dinner one night to celebrate his team winning the championship in football. Everybody got dressed up to go to this fancy restaurant. John decided that he was too tired after a hard game to shower and change, so he went as he was. His mother tried to get him to change, but he insisted that no one would notice his dirty pants and shirt. He even smelled a little bit. But his mother said, "Okay, this is your day." When they arrived at the restaurant, the host informed them that

John couldn't come in because of the way he looked. John became angry. He couldn't understand why they wouldn't let him in. They called the manager over, and the manager explained that this was the restaurant's policy. This was a fancy restaurant, and customers must dress a certain way to get in. He told them that everybody could come in except John. The family was very disappointed, because this was a celebration for John, and it wouldn't be the same without him. So they decided to go home.

Before we are saved, we are like John. We are not fit to enter heaven because of our sin. The rest of John's family was prepared to enter the restaurant, but he wasn't.

Do you want to be like John's family–ready for heaven–or like John–ready for hell? The Bible tells us that those who are not saved will not enter heaven. When we are saved, we will live with God forever. If you are not saved, you will live in hell forever.

Why Do We Need to Be Saved?

Think About It

Parent/Teacher:

- Share what is special about your best friend.
- Share how you have established a relationship with Jesus.

Children:

- What did you learn about God?
- Did you learn anything new?
- Why couldn't John get into the restaurant?
- Do you need to be saved?

Key Verse

For all have sinned and fall short of the glory of God.
(Rom. 3:23, NIV)

Prayer Time

Dear God, I know that I am dirty, a sinner. Help me to understand that I need to be saved. Amen.

Chapter 11
Benefits to Being Saved

Some of you are probably thinking that life will not be fun after you become saved. This is far from the truth. Life is so much better when you become saved. You can still go to parties, have wonderful friends, and play sports. The only thing that changes is how you act while you are doing these things.

Being saved is so awesome. Before I was saved, I worried about a lot of things. I didn't know how to pick good friends, so I was mistreated by my friends. I didn't have anyone to really talk to about my problems, and now I have Jesus. I did bad things and had to suffer the bad consequences.

This is why I am writing to young people. I want you to understand the importance of becoming saved while you are young. Being saved has been the best part of my life. I have to tell you that being saved may not remove the mean people from your life, it may not stop your parents from arguing, and it may not help you do well on a test. Being saved does promise the following:

1. **Eternal life.** You will live in heaven forever with God.

2. **Friendship with Jesus.** Jesus promises us a friendship that will last forever. We can tell Him all of our problems.

Ashley, saved at age 9. She says being saved has made her want to draw closer to Jesus.

Benefits to Being Saved

3. **God's grace and mercy.** God will forgive us when we make mistakes, even though we do not deserve it.

These are only three of the benefits of being saved. The most important one is that you will live with God forever in heaven. Some of you may be thinking, *What is so great about heaven?* Well, the Bible tells us that this is where all of those who believe in Jesus Christ will live. Wouldn't it be great to live with people who want only to worship God? In heaven, no one will get sick. People will not argue or tease you. You can run around with the most dangerous animals, and they will not harm you. I've always wanted to pet a tiger, and in heaven I will get a chance to do that. My children are always saying that they are bored. You will not get bored in heaven. Heaven will be like going to an amusement park. You will have to pay a fee to get in, but once you get in, it is so much fun.

Did You Know?

- Your cereal is made from grass. Most cereal is made from grass like rice, wheat, barley, or corn. The grass outside on the ground is made for wild animals and not for us.

Think About It

Parent/Teacher:

- Share how your life changed after being saved.

Children:

- What did you learn about God?
- If you could make heaven anyway you wanted, what would it be like?
- Look up the following scriptures to learn about heaven: Rev. 21:25-27, 22:3-4; 2 Cor. 4:18, 5:2-3, 15:53; Isa. 11:9, 29:18.

Key Verse

In my Father's house are many rooms; if it were not so, I would have told you. I am going there to prepare a place for you.
(John 14:2, NIV)

Prayer Time

Dear God, help me focus on what I will get in heaven and not on what I want here on earth. Amen.

Benefits to Being Saved

Play It Again #2

Do you remember what you read? Answer the questions below to see how much you know.

1. When are you in God's circle of protection?

    _____ a. When you are doing what you want

    _____ b. When you disobey your parents

    _____ c. When you obey God

2. When is it most difficult for you to make right choices?

3. Do you have friends that are making the right choices?

4. What are the consequences of sin?

    _____ a. Reward

    _____ b. Punishment

    _____ c. Fun

5. Is disobeying your parents a sin?

    _____ a. Yes   _____ b. No

6. How do you learn about all of God's rules?

Bible Quiz #2

How well do you know the Bible? Try to answer the questions yourself. The Bible verse is listed if you need help.

1. Who ate the fruit first (Gen. 3:6)?

    _____ a. Eve

    _____ b. Adam

2. What happened to Adam and Eve after they ate the fruit (Gen. 3:23)?

    _____ a. God ignored their sin.

    _____ b. God just talked to them.

    _____ c. God kicked them out of the Garden of Eden.

3. What did God put in front of the Garden of Eden to keep Adam and Eve out (Gen. 3:24)?

4. Abel attended sheep, what did Cain do (Gen. 4:2)?

    _____ a. Fished

    _____ b. Farmed

    _____ c. Raised cows

Benefits to Being Saved

Fun Time #2

Unscramble the Bible verse Prov. 10:8 (NASB), below to learn what happens to those who do not follow God's rules.

_____	_____	_____
eht	esiw	fo

_____	_____
treah	lliw

_____	_____
eviecer	sdnammoc

_____	_____
tub	a

_____	_____	_____
gnilbbab	loof	lliw

_____	_____
eb	deniur.

My Child's Heart

Fun Time

Find the words that keep us out of the circle of safety.

```
G B E E U R K V H C J J K A
N E J C W N I M A D E W N L S
I U S N L Q K T V A T G K S I
Y M S E Y M I I L J N V E U T
L C E I P N G O N I Q N H W V
G O N D G R U A T D H N O Q W
O V I E V S J H G S N E X U M
S E Z B Y F G N I L A E T S R
S T A O R I I F J K F U S Z B
I I L S F A L U H Q V T L S E
P N E I I E C H E A T I N G U
I G W D S T U B B O R N E S S
N Q Z X I O X Y R G N A S Q X
G M J S V R K M W E F D C B A
H X Z J D C P S S U M S N I F
```

ANGRY
CHEATING
COVETING
DISOBEDIENCE
FIGHTING
GOSSIPING
HATING
JEALOUSY
LAZINESS
LYING
PRIDE
SELFISHNESS
STEALING
STUBBORNESS
UNKINDNESS

PART III
My Salvation

Chapter 12
Jesus Is Our Superhero

Jesus is our superhero. He is more powerful than any of the superheroes on television. He came down from heaven with His super-saving powers. What is so super about Jesus? He was born a mighty king with the unique power to save everybody. The superheroes on television have nothing compared to Jesus. He can walk through steel doors, and He can heal the hurt and sick. He knows what everyone is thinking, so He can come up with the best defenses. He is stronger than man or thing. He is so strong that not even Satan can tempt Him. Unlike our television superheroes, Jesus has the ability to save and protect everybody all at once. He doesn't need anyone else's help. He has enough power within himself to do it all. With a superhero like this, who needs anyone else? Jesus is all we need to be saved. He is the only way to salvation.

In John 14:6 (NIV), "Jesus answered, '*I am the way and the truth and the life. No one comes to the Father except through me.*'" God tells us that Jesus is the only way to Him because of our sin. Jesus died for our sins so that we could be reconciled with God. *Reconcile* means mending a broken relationship. Now we can be God's friend again.

Jesus told a story about ten virgins who went out with their lamps to meet the bridegroom. Five of the women were foolish because

My Child's Heart

they did not take along oil for their lamps, but the other five did. It took a long time for the bridegroom to come, so the virgins without oil had to leave and go find oil. The bridegroom came while they were gone. The virgins with oil were able to go into the wedding banquet. This story tells us that we need to be saved today.

No one knows when Jesus will return. No one knows when he or she is going to die. It is important that we are saved before these things happen. Are you ready for Jesus? Are you saved?

Jesus Is Our Superhero

Think About It

Parent/Teacher:

- Share with your child a time when you did not listen to God and the consequence.
- Discuss some things that you can do to enhance your relationship with Jesus.

Children:

- What is the only way to get to God?
- Why can we not get to God ourselves?
- What can you do to get to know Jesus better?

Key Verse

And whoever lives and believes in me will never die. Do you believe this?

(John 11:26, NIV)

Prayer Time

Dear God, help me understand that Jesus is the only way to heaven. Nothing else will get me to heaven, not even being good. Amen.

Chapter 13
Children Need To Be Saved

You are never too young to have a relationship with God. Find Matthew 19:13-15 and read it to your parents. You see, God designed heaven for children and adults. He expects people to become saved as children and understand what it means to be saved. I was baptized at the age of 6, but I didn't understand what this meant until I was an adult. I said the words, "I believe that Jesus Christ is Lord and Savior." However, I was just saying some words. The pastor told me to say it, and I did. I should have asked what it meant, but I didn't. I didn't realize that I was supposed to start doing what the Bible tells us to do.

Children are not automatically saved because of their age. Once you are old enough to understand sin and the Word of God, you will be held accountable. That means that you are responsible for the things you do. What you do as a child matters to God. The reward for being saved and following God is eternal life in heaven. This means that after you die, you will live in heaven with God forever. However, when you do not make a decision to be saved at a young age, you will go through life making a lot of mistakes. You will sin all of the time. The consequences of your sins will make you unhappy.

My Child's Heart

Jesus tells us in Mark 8 that anyone who does not follow Him will be turned away from the gates of heaven.

Just like Adam and Eve were turned away from the Garden of Eden, children will be turned away from heaven if they have not accepted Jesus Christ as Lord and Savior. Babies and small children will go to heaven because they are not old enough to understand sin. We are old enough to understand about God when we are about six years old.

We do not know when Jesus will come back to get all those who are saved or when we will die. It may be when you are a child, so get ready today, and don't wait until you are a grownup.

Children Need To Be Saved

Think About It

Parent/Teacher:

- Did you become saved as a child?
- Discuss with your children the benefits of being saved at an early age.

Children:

- What did you learn about God?
- Did you learn anything new?
- Will children go to hell if they are not saved?

Key Verse

Jesus said, "Let the little children come to me, and do not hinder them, for the kingdom of heaven belongs to such as these."
(Matt. 19:14, NIV)

Prayer Time

Dear God, help me understand the importance of coming to you as a child. Amen.

Chapter 14
What If I Sin After I am Saved?

You are not expected to stop sinning before you can become saved. And you are not expected to stop sinning the day you become saved. Being saved is like getting your training wheels off your bike. You are excited, because this means you are growing up. But you are also afraid, because now you have to learn how to ride it. Your parents start you off by holding the back of your seat until you balance. When they feel like you are balanced, they will let go. Guess what happens? You fall. You keep trying until you get better and better at balancing. Eventually you are riding like a pro.

After you are saved, you will still make mistakes and sin, but you have to keep trying. You should feel bad about the sin. If you get angry with someone one day and push them, this does not mean you are not saved. You have just made a mistake. This mistake will probably lead to a punishment. If you push someone every day just for fun or to hurt them, you have to ask yourself if you are saved.

You will have to work every day to remove sin from your life. You will find it easier to stop sinning when you go to Sunday School regularly and read the Bible and other Christian books. So don't give up. Keep working to get rid of your sins. Pray and ask God to help you. He is faithful and will help you stop.

My daughter had a bad habit of biting the skin on her fingers when she was nervous or bored. She seemed to bite them more during school. No matter what we did, she would not stop biting her fingers. School was about to start up again, so I asked her to pray every day for God to help her to stop. She did not stop overnight. But after about a week of praying and asking God to help her, she stopped. She comes home every day from school and tells us that she did not bite her fingers. God answered her prayers. God can and will help you to stop doing things that are not good.

What If I Sin After I am Saved?

THINK ABOUT IT

Parent/Teacher:

- Share with your child how you continued to make mistakes after you were saved.
- Tell them how you continue to love them even when they make mistakes.

Children:

- Share your feelings about being saved.
- Are you afraid to be saved?
- If you are saved, what are your concerns?

Key Verse

Don't let evil defeat you, but defeat evil with good.
(Rom. 12:21, CEV)

Prayer Time

Dear God, please help me know the things I am doing that are wrong. Help me not do them. Amen.

Chapter 15
Believe that Jesus is Lord

The first thing we must do to be saved is believe and confess that Jesus is Lord. We have to believe in our hearts and say out loud to someone that Jesus is God. We know we have to do this because Romans 10:9-10 tell us this: "*So you will be saved, if you honestly say, 'Jesus is Lord,' and if you believe with all your heart that God raised him from death. God will accept you and save you, if you truly believe this and tell it to others*" (CEV).

The Bible tells us that Jesus is Lord and that He was raised from the dead. Everything in the Bible is true. God told the people who wrote the Bible what to write, just like He gave Moses the Ten Commandments.

You should always check to see if what people are telling you is in the Bible. So open your Bibles to the following verse to see that God tells us that Jesus is Lord.

"*The high priest said to him, 'I charge you under oath by the living God: Tell us if you are the Christ, the Son of God.' 'Yes, it is as you say,' Jesus replied. 'But I say to all of you: In the future you will see the Son of Man sitting at the right hand of the Mighty One and coming on the clouds of heaven'*" (Matt. 26:63b-64, NIV). Jesus tells us in the Bible that He is not an ordinary person but the true Son of God.

My Child's Heart

Turn in your Bibles to Matthew 20:17-19 to confirm that Jesus rose from the dead. *"Now as Jesus was going up to Jerusalem, he took the twelve disciples aside and said to them, 'We are going up to Jerusalem, and the Son of Man will be betrayed to the chief priests and the teachers of the law. They will condemn him to death and will turn him over to the Gentiles to be mocked and flogged and crucified. On the third day he will be raised to life!'"* (Matt. 20:17-19, NIV).

Go to John 14:6 and fill in the blanks below.

I am the _____ and the _____ and the _____

No _____ comes to the _____ except _____ Me.

There are many religions today, but only by believing that Jesus is the Son of God and Lord and Savior will you get to heaven. Nothing else will do it, not even being good and doing good things.

Believe that Jesus is Lord

Think About It

Parent/Teacher:

- Have you said out loud and told anyone that you believe that Jesus is Lord?
- Do you believe that Jesus has been raised from the dead?
- Tell someone about Jesus this week.

Children:

- Have you said out loud and told anyone that you believe that Jesus is Lord?
- Do you believe that Jesus has been raised from the dead?
- If you believe that Jesus is Lord and Savior, say it out loud right now.
- Tell a friend about Jesus this week.

Key Verse

Jesus answered, "I am the way and the truth and the life."
(John 14:6a, NIV)

Prayer Time

Dear God, please help me believe in you and trust you all of the time. Amen.

Chapter 16
Tell God What You Have Done

The second thing we must do to be saved is to confess our sins and ask for forgiveness. The Bible tells us in 1 John 1:9 (NIV),"*If we confess our sins, he is faithful and just and will forgive us our sins and purify us from all unrighteousness.*"

Confess means to:

    A: Admit that your sin is wrong and that it is not pleasing to God.

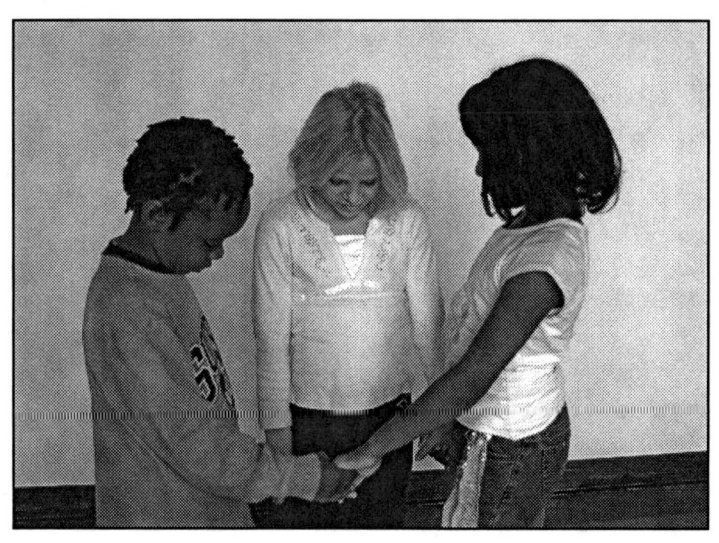

B: Tell God about the bad things you have done and ask for forgiveness.

Repent means to:

- A. Turn away from your sin.
- B. Be sorry for what you have done.
- C. Promise not to do it again.

When we ask God to forgive us for hitting our big sister, we are telling God that we will no longer do this. When we confess our sins, the Holy Spirit will come and help us stop. You may give in to temptation and hit her again one day, but you should not be hitting her all of the time. When you do slip up, remember to ask for forgiveness by praying and asking God to help you with this. You can stop hitting her!

Tell God What You Have Done

THINK ABOUT IT

Parent/Teacher:

- Write down the things that you do that are not pleasing to God.
- Share the appropriate things with your children. Ask God to forgive you.

Children:

- What did you learn about God?
  Make a list of the sins you need God to forgive (example: lying, stealing, saying unkind words, not sharing).

    1. _____
    2. _____
    3. _____

Key Verse

If we confess our sins, he is faithful and just and will forgive us our sins and purify us from all unrighteousness.

(1 John 1:9, NIV)

Prayer Time

Dear God, help me know when I have sinned, to feel bad about my sins, and to turn away from my sins. Amen.

Chapter 17
Do Things God's Way

Thirdly, we need to decide to be obedient to all of God's commands. We must make Jesus Lord over our lives. Believing that Jesus is Lord and Savior is not enough. We must live a life that is pleasing to God. Satan knows that Jesus is Lord and Savior, but he has not made Christ the Lord over his life. So Satan is not saved.

In the case of the puppy, the owner is lord over the puppy. The puppy has to do what you tell it to do. The puppy's job is to follow your rules. The puppy can no longer be concerned about what he wants but what you, as his owner, wants.

Jesus is Lord over your life when you do what He says. If the puppy was owned by someone else before you got it, it may have some behaviors that you do not like. The first owner may have allowed the puppy to jump on the sofa and sleep in the bed. Now you are the owner. You do not like these things, so the puppy must change. We are like the puppy; we have bad behaviors that are not acceptable to God. Since God is our new owner, He expects us to stop them and be more like Christ. Changing these behaviors is proof that Christ is Lord over your life. It shows God that you are no longer in control of your life.

Steps to Salvation

- Believe in your heart that Jesus is Lord.
- Confess your sins and repent.
- Do things God's way. Make Jesus Lord over your life, and be obedient.

Are you saved? Can you be called a Christian? You do not have to wait until you are an adult. You don't have to be perfect. You can become saved even though you still sin. In fact, you cannot stop sinning until you are saved. If you are afraid, you are not alone. Pray and ask God to remove your fear. He is faithful and will listen to your prayers.

Do Things God's Way

Think About It

Parent/Teacher:

- Have you decided to make Christ Lord of your life?
- Share with your children a time when you put God first in your life, though it wasn't easy.
- Share with your child a time when they obeyed you quickly and how this made you feel.

Children:

- Have you decided to make Christ Lord of your life? If not, why not?
- If God is Lord over your life, what kinds of words should come out of your mouth?
- If God is Lord over your life, how should you treat others?
- If God is Lord over your life, should you do only things that make you happy?

Key Verse

"If you really knew me, you would know my Father as well. From now on, you do know him and have seen him."
(John 14:7, NIV)

Prayer Time

Dear God, help me to put you first in my life. Amen.

Chapter 18
Just Say These Words

You are probably thinking that being saved will be hard, and your friends will laugh at you. Don't worry; God will take care of you. You may lose some friends, but you will gain a loving Father and many more Christian friends. The great thing is that you do not have to worry about God turning away from you. He loves you no matter what you do.

To become saved, say the prayer below and mean it:

Dear Jesus, I believe that you are the Son of God and that you died on the cross to forgive me of my sins. I know I am a sinner, and I can do nothing to make up for my sins, but you loved me enough to die on the cross in my place. Please forgive me of my past sins (name some of your sins). Thank you for loving me. I pray that you will wash me clean today so that I will put you first in my life and do what you want and not what I want to do. I ask the Holy Spirit to come into my life and guide me in this new life of serving you. Amen.

If you prayed this today, please fill in the date. _____

In our salvation prayer, we asked God to forgive us of our sins. The Bible tells us, *"For all have sinned and fall short of the glory of*

God" (Rom. 3:23, NIV). *"But God demonstrates His own love for us in this: While we were still sinners, Christ died for us"* (Rom. 5:8, NIV). Isn't it great to know that we can be saved while we are still sinners? This is what God calls mercy and grace. People may not always show you mercy, but God will show mercy all of the time. Mercy is the forgiveness, kindness, and love that people show you when you make a mistake. We don't have to stop doing all of those bad things before we are saved. Once we get the Holy Spirit, we will be able to stop those bad things.

Markell, saved at age 8.

Just Say These Words

When Jesus Christ died on the cross for us, He was sinless and took on our sins. Sin pays off with death. Death is a separation from God. But God's gift is eternal life given by Jesus Christ our Lord (Rom. 6:23). We deserve to be punished for our sins, but Christ takes that punishment for us. Since Christ takes our punishment for us, we must ask for forgiveness for our sins prior to being saved and after we are saved.

Salvation frees us from the punishment of sin. If you said the prayer above, jump up and down and shout, "Thank you, God!" God tells us once we have prayed this prayer, we should be baptized. Talk to your parents about baptism.

Think About It

Parent/Teacher:

- If your children have decided to become saved, congratulate them. Tell them that this is the most important decision they will ever make. Have a salvation party.
- Give them a token to remind them of this decision. Visit my website for awesome jewelry designed just for "My Child's Heart" participants.
- Visit my website to print off a commitment contract that can be posted in their rooms as a reminder. This commitment contract is also available at the end of the book.
- If your child has not decided to turn his or her life over to God, do not put pressure on the child. Continue to pray with your child that God will soften his or her heart for Him.

Children:

- Since you are a sinner, have you accepted Jesus Christ as your Lord and Savior?
- Is there anyone who has not sinned?
- Can you go to heaven by just being good?
- Are you afraid to follow God?
- Do you have to be perfect to be saved?
- Can you be a sinner and still be saved?
- If you have not decided to become saved, what is preventing you from becoming a Christian?

Key Verse

For the wages of sin is death, but the gift of God is eternal life in Christ Jesus our Lord.

(Rom. 6:23, NIV)

Prayer Time

Dear God, help me open my heart to you as a child. Amen.

Just Say These Words

Play It Again #3

Do you remember what you read? Answer the questions below to see how much you know.

1. You can know for sure that you are a Christian if:

   _____ a. You treat others kindly.

   _____ b. You go to church.

   _____ c. You believe in your heart that Jesus is Lord, have repented of your sins and asked for forgiveness, have made Christ Lord over your life, and live in obedience.

   _____ d. You know that Jesus Christ is Lord.

   _____ e. Your parents are Christians.

Did you check answer C? Salvation is only promised if you decided to do all of answer C.

2. God rules are made to

   _____ a. Keep us from having fun.

   _____ b. Make us unhappy.

   _____ c. Make us sin.

   _____ d. Protect us.

3. Is there any other god besides God?

   _____ a. Yes   _____ b. No

4. Is there anything that God cannot do?

   _____ a. Yes   _____ b. No

BIBLE QUIZ #3

(Battle Your Parents)

1. What was the name of Adam and Eve's third son (Gen. 5:3)?

    _____ a. Cain

    _____ b. Abel

    _____ c. Seth

2. How old was Adam when he died (Gen. 5:5)?

    _____ a. 930 years old

    _____ b. 600 years old

    _____ c. 800 years old

3. Who moved upon the face of a dark and formless world (Gen. 1:1)?

4. God created the world in ____ days and rested on ____ day (Gen. 1:27-2:3).

5. Why did God kick Adam and Eve out of the garden (Gen. 3:22-23)?

6. Complete: For God so loved the world that he gave his only begotten Son, that whosoever believeth in him should not perish but have_____ (John 3:16).

Just Say These Words

Fun Time #3

Write out the statement below using the number grid. Each number has a matching letter.

A	B	C	D	E	F	G	H	I	J	K	L	M
1	2	3	4	5	6	7	8	9	10	11	12	13

N	O	P	Q	R	S	T	U	V	W	X	Y	Z
14	15	16	17	18	19	20	21	22	23	24	25	26

_____   _____
2 5 12 9 5 22 5   20 8 1 20

_____   _____
10 5 19 21 19   9 19

_____
12 15 18 4

Fun Time

Unscramble 2 John 6 below to see what Jesus would love for a gift.

sihT	si	evol
taht	ew	klaw
ni	ecneidebo	
ot	sih	
	sdnammoc	

Just Say These Words

Fun Time

How many words can you and your parents make from the word below (you should be able to find at least 16 words)?

Salvation

Saint	
_____	_____
_____	_____
_____	_____
_____	_____
_____	_____
_____	_____
_____	_____
_____	_____

PART IV
My Life After I Am Saved

Chapter 19
Jesus Can Help Me Stop Doing Bad Things

John was nine years old and a really good kid. He tried to do the right thing but couldn't all of the time. Every night he counted his sins. After doing this for a month, he realized he always had the same five sins on his list. His common sins list looked like this:

John's Sin List

1. I didn't share with my sister.
2. I become angry and sad every time I lost in a game.
3. I complained when my mother told me to go to bed.
4. I talked in class after my teacher told me to be quiet.
5. I didn't tell the truth because I thought I would get into trouble.

No matter what he did, he always had at least one of these sins on his list.

Did You Know?

If John had only these five sins on his list every day for one week, he would have 35 sins (5 sins times 7 days=35) at the end of the week.

My Child's Heart

How many sins would he have at the end of one year? You are correct if your answer is 1,820 sins (35 sins every week times 52 weeks in a year=1,820).

Every year John has at least 1,820 sins. Holy Moses, that is a lot. How many sins do you think you have every week? What do you think John could do to stop doing those bad things? You are right if you said he could accept Jesus Christ as Lord and Savior.

John decided to accept Jesus Christ into his life when he turned ten. When he did this, the Holy Spirit came to live within him. You

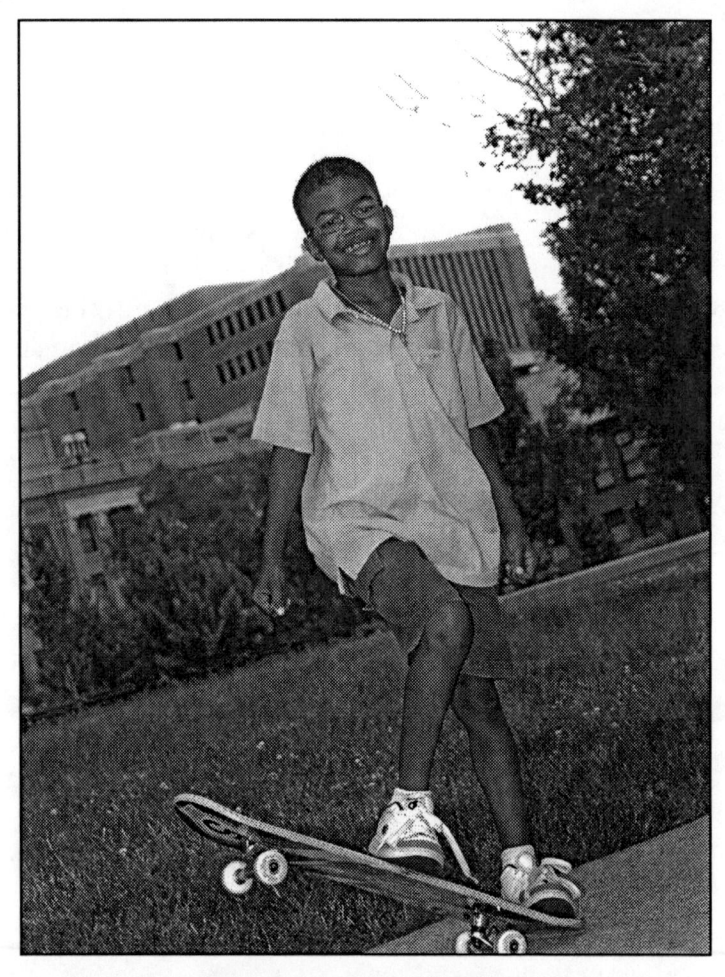

Cameron, saved at age 7. Cameron says,
"Being saved is the right thing to do."

Jesus Can Help Me Stop Doing Bad Things

know the Holy Spirit reminds us to do the right thing. The Holy Spirit is like a cheerleader. He cheers when you do the right thing. He also tells you when you do something wrong.

After John accepted Jesus Christ, he felt terrible about doing those bad things. After about six months, he realized that he had stopped getting angry when he lost a game. He also noticed that when he stopped getting mad, he began to win more often.

Now he had only four sins that he did all of the time. John felt so good about this change in himself. John knew that God would be pleased with him for getting rid of one sin. He knew that when he got to heaven God would discuss his sins with him. John did not want God to be disappointed in him. John also knew that the rewards in heaven are based on the things he did on earth after he was saved. John wanted to get many rewards in heaven, so he knew he must stop doing these sins.

As John continued to try to please God, he was able to stop arguing with his parents when they told him to go to bed. John was pleased again about this, because he knew that God blesses us when we do not sin.

By the time John was 13 years old, he had stopped doing all of the things on his list. He was proud of his progress. He knew that God was pleased with him, because God does not like it when we continue to do the same sin over and over again. John continued to keep this list of sins, and sometimes these old sins would be on the list. But John was happy that they were only on the list one time in the whole month instead of every day.

There are many benefits to being saved as a child:

1. You will be ready when Jesus comes.
2. You will go to heaven when you die.
3. God will bless you when you are saved.
4. You will have more rewards in heaven if you start being obedient to God as a child.
5. You can reduce your total sins.
6. You will reduce the number of bad consequences because of your sins.

Think About It

Parent/Teacher:

- Tell of a time you had to do something that was hard.
- Share with your children other stories that will show them the importance of following God.

Children:

- Start a sin checklist. Every day before you go to bed, write down your sins to see if you have some common ones. Pray and ask God to help you stop these sins.

Key Verse

Rejoice and be glad, because great is your reward in heaven.
(Matt. 5:12a NIV)

Prayer Time

Dear God, thank you for rewarding me for my obedience. Help me do what is right. Amen.

Chapter 20
Love Gifts from Jesus

A friend is someone who is very special to you–someone you like being around a lot. Close friends normally give each other gifts, especially on birthdays. Jesus loves us so much that He gave us a gift before we were born. He wants us to be with Him in heaven, so He took our sin punishment. We deserve to die for our sins, but He died on the cross for us instead. Jesus paid our price for us!

Let's say you stole a basketball from the store. The manager catches you, and you go to jail. Once in jail, a court date will be scheduled to determine the punishment for the crime. The judge decides that you will have to pay $500 or go to jail for three months. Unfortunately, you do not have $500. Out of the blue, a man comes up and pays your $500 fine. You are free and clear. The store will no longer punish you for this crime.

This is what Jesus did for us. The Bible tells us, "*For the wages of sin is death*" (Rom. 6:23, NIV). He paid our death fine for us when He died on the cross. We can now have a relationship with God. What a great gift!

Since Jesus is no longer on earth, He wanted us to have something that would remind us of Him. So He gives us the Holy Spirit as a friendship gift. When we become saved, the Holy Spirit comes to live in us, and we start a new life. We are born again. You are probably thinking, *Born again. Can we be born twice?* No, this born again comes from a washing that goes on in our hearts after we accept Jesus Christ as Lord. *"But now the name of our Lord Jesus Christ and the power of God's Spirit have washed you and made you holy and acceptable to God"* (1 Cor. 6:11b, CEV). When we are born again, we receive eternal life.

Jaz'min, saved at age 12, and Jaire, saved at age 8.

A person with eternal life will live forever with God in heaven.

If you came into the house all dirty after playing a game or sport, your mother would probably tell you not to sit on anything but to go straight to the bathroom and take a bath. Bathing cleanses you, and then you are able to sit on the furniture or your bed. Before your bath, you couldn't do this. This is what the Holy Spirit does. It cleanses us so we will be obedient to God. The Holy Spirit helps us stop sinning. Remember, everything doesn't change overnight, so be patient, and don't give up.

Love Gifts from Jesus

Think About It

Parent/Teacher:

- Share how the Holy Spirit keeps you from doing the wrong thing.
- Share something that you have stopped doing since you have been saved.

Children:

- What did you learn about God?
- How do you feel about what Jesus did for you?
- Have you told Him this? If not, do it today.
- Have you given Jesus a friendship gift? Cross out all of the letters "z," to see what you can give Jesus as a gift.

Lozve the Lzord your Gzod with all of your hezart and with all your szoul and with all your strezngth.
(Deut, 6:5 NIV)

Key Verse

Believe in the Lord Jesus and you will be saved.
(Acts 16:31, NIV)

Prayer Time

Dear God, help me trust in You and make Jesus my friend. Amen.

Chapter 21

What Do I Do After I Sin?

Although God sees everything that we do, we must still confess our sins and ask for forgiveness. He wants us to admit what we have done. When Adam and Eve sinned, what did they do? Let's go back to our story. *"The woman stared at the fruit. It looked beautiful and tasty. She wanted the wisdom that it would give her, and she ate some of the fruit. Her husband was there with her, so she gave some to him, and he ate it too. Right away they saw what they had done, and they realized they were naked. Then they sewed fig leaves together to make something to cover themselves. Late in the afternoon a breeze began to blow, and the man and woman heard the* Lord God *walking in the garden. They were frightened and hid behind some trees"* (Gen. 3:6-8, CEV).

Adam and Eve hid because they had sinned. Do you try to hide your sins by blaming someone else or by lying? Well, Adam and Eve tried to hide from their sin, but God already knew about it. We cannot hide from God. Remember, He knows everything.

Have you ever wondered how your parents know what you are doing or have done without being there? Well, God tells your parents or others. I was driving in the car the other day, and my children were riding in the back seat. I told them to stop throwing crackers. My son quickly responded, "How did you know without looking that we were doing that?" I told him that God gives parents wisdom.

So when you do something wrong, don't try to hide it. Just confess what you have done to an adult and to God. Remember, if you do not admit to your wrongdoings, such as hurting someone's feelings, not sharing, stealing, or talking badly about someone, God will not forgive you. God will forgive our sins over and over and over again if we confess. The Bible tell us, "*But if we confess our sins to God, he can always be trusted to forgive us and take our sins away*" (1 John 1:9, CEV). Remember, to confess means to tell God that what you did is wrong. He will never stop forgiving us when we confess and repent. Repent means to stop doing it. God expects us to stop sinning when we repent of that sin.

Wow, when we ask God to help us with our sins, He will help us to stop. All sin can be stopped with God's help. Remember, John couldn't stop sinning until he accepted Jesus Christ as Lord. God will help you stop doing bad things as well. Just pray and ask for help.

What Do I Do After I Sin?

Think About It

Parent/Teacher:

- Ask your children to forgive you for something you did wrong to them individually. This is an opportunity for you to show them how easy it is to ask for forgiveness. Maybe you spoke harshly to them, made a promise that you didn't keep, or neglected to spend quality time with them.

Children:

- What must we do when we sin? Must we ask God for forgiveness every time we sin?
- Ask your parents for forgiveness. Maybe you didn't clean your room when they asked, ate something you were not supposed to eat, or disobeyed them some other way.

Key Verse

If we confess our sins, He is faithful and just and will forgive us ours sins and purify us from all righteous.
(1 John 1:9, CEV)

Prayer Time

Dear God, thank you for sending your Son Jesus Christ so that I may be forgiven by you. Amen.

Chapter 22
How Does God Forgive?

How God forgives you depends on how well you forgive others. *"Whenever you stand up to pray, you must forgive what others have done to you. Then your Father in heaven will forgive your sins"* (Mark 11:25, CEV). *"If you forgive others for the wrongs they do to you, your Father in heaven will forgive you"* (Matt. 6:14, CEV). We must ask God to forgive us for our sins. We also must forgive those who treat us badly. You have to forgive a classmate for stealing your pencil, someone for pushing you, and someone who calls you a bad name. Forgiveness is changing bad thoughts about someone to good thoughts. The forgiveness must be sincere.

SINCERE FORGIVENESS MEANS...

1. That you will not hold this against them later.
2. You will not remind them of this sin.
3. You will not share this sin with others.
4. You will not try to get even with them because of this sin.
5. You will not carry this hurt around with you.

The disciple Peter asked Jesus, "How many times are we to forgive someone?" Jesus answered, "Not seven times but 70 times seven" (Matt. 18:21-22, NLT). Have you ever had to forgive someone 490 times? Probably not, so keep on forgiving them. Wow, God expects a lot from us, doesn't He? Don't be afraid. You can do this with the help of the Holy Spirit!

Did You Know?

There are 27 books in the New Testament, and Paul wrote 15 of these books. Paul's original name was Saul, and he killed Christians before he became a Christian. God allows even those who have killed His children to become Christians. So don't think that God will not accept you into His family.

How Does God Forgive?

Think About It

Parent/Teacher:

- Share a time when you had to forgive someone who hurt you.
- Was it easy to forgive this person?

Children:

- Name someone who has hurt you that you need to forgive.
- What are you going to do to forgive this person?
- How will you show this person that you have forgiven him or her?
- God still loves you even when you make mistakes. How does that make you feel?

Key Verse

Bear with each other and forgive whatever grievance you may have against one another. Forgive as the Lord forgave you.

(Col. 3:13, NIV)

Prayer Time

Dear God, please help me forgive those who mistreat me. Amen.

Chapter 23
Find a Christian Mentor and Christian Friends

Once you are saved, please find a Christian mentor. The world tells us that we need a mentor for sports and other activities, but what about one to help us grow close to Christ? A Christian mentor is someone who has been following Christ for a long time–someone who can help answer your questions about Christianity. This person is someone who is trying to be obedient to God. You can avoid many painful experiences by learning from someone who has been following Christ longer than you.

A Christian mentor should be someone who reads and studies the Bible daily. He or she attends church regularly and is involved in the church. This person will have asked God to take control of his or her life. Paul was the new church mentor. Your mentor can be a godly parent, relative, or adult friend. If you choose someone who is not your parent, tell your parents that you have chosen this person as a mentor.

Talk to your mentor or godly parent when you have questions about the Bible or need someone to help you make a choice. Before you go to your mentor, always pray first, and ask God to give you, your parents, and the mentor wisdom.

Mentors are great, but Christian friends are even better. Christian friends are important because they can help you be obedient to

God. Make sure your friends are trying to please God. Remember, everybody who claims to be a Christian is not a Christian. Join Sunday School, or get together with a small group of Christians your age. Invite your friends to study my other books with you and your parents. Following God is easier and more fun when you do it with friends. *"Therefore encourage one another and build up one another"* (1 Thess. 5:11a, NASB).

Find a Christian Mentor and Christian Friends

Think About It

Parents/Teacher:

- Discuss how your mentors and friends help you to obey God.

Children:

- Who will be your mentor? Remember to talk this over with your parents.
- Who will be your friend to help you be obedient to God? Ask your parents to help you choose someone.

Key Verse

He who walks with the wise grows wise.

(Prov. 13:20a, NIV)

Prayer Time

Dear God, give me wisdom when it comes to selecting my mentor and Christian friends. Amen.

Chapter 24
Myths About Being Saved

We have learned many new things about what it means to be saved. Here are some lies about what it means to be saved:

Lie # 1: Good people will go to heaven. No one is good; all have sinned. Being a good person does not make you a Christian. Doing good things will not get you into heaven. We are not saved because we do good things but because of God's grace. However, once we are saved, God expects us to do good things.

Lie # 2: Attending church will get me into heaven. Church attendance is important, but it does not make you saved. There are many people who go to church, but they are not saved, and you can tell by their behavior–the things they do or don't do.

Lie # 3: All religions lead to heaven. Not all people believe in the God of our Bible. Many people believe in a different god. There are many different religions in our world. Religion does not make you saved. There is only one way to heaven and that is to believe that Jesus Christ is the Son of God, Savior, and God.

Lie # 4: Speaking in tongues means I am saved. God gives each of us a special gift. Speaking in tongues is a special gift that He gives to some people. Speaking in tongues is a special language that

God gives some of us when we speak to Him. Speaking in tongues is not a sign of being saved or necessary to be saved.

Lie # 5: Baptism will save you. Baptism is something that God commands us to do after we are saved. Baptism does not save us. It shows the world that we were sinners and the Holy Spirit washed us clean when we accepted Jesus Christ. *"Whoever believes and is baptized will be saved, but whoever does not believe will be condemned"* (Mark 16:16a, NIV).

Myths About Being Saved

Think About It

Parent/Teacher/Children:

- Write down anything new that you have learned or want to remember.
- Fill in the blanks for Ephesians 2:8-9, NIV. You may look up the scripture in your Bible for help.

For it is by _____ (gcrae) you have been _____ ___ (svead), through _____ (fitah) and this not from yourselves, it is the _____ (gfit) of God not by _____, (skrow), so that no one can boast.

Key Verse

My soul glorifies the Lord and my spirit rejoices in God my Savior.
(Luke 1:46-47, NIV)

Prayer Time

Dear God, thank you for giving me the understanding of salvation. Amen.

Play It Again #4

1. Who wants to have a relationship with you?_____

2. Who broke the relationship with God?

    _____ a. Seth

    _____ b. Noah

    _____ c. Adam and Eve

3. Who made it possible for us to have a relationship with God again?

    _____ a. Jesus

    _____ b. Adam

    _____ c. Abraham

4. Who can have a relationship with God?

    _____ a. Those who go to church.

    _____ b. Those who have heard about God.

    _____ c. Those who are saved.

5. What must you do when you sin?

6. Why is it important to forgive others?

Myths About Being Saved

Bible Quiz #4

(Test your parent's knowledge of the Bible)

1. What is Ruth's mother in law's name (Ruth 1:1-5)?

   _____ a. Mary   _____ b. Naomi   _____ c. Janah

2. What man was asked to sacrifice his son (Gen. 22:1-2)?

   _____ a. Noah   _____ b. Abraham   _____ c. Isaac

3. Who had twelve sons (Gen. 35:22)?

   _____ a. John   _____ b. Isaac   _____ c. Jacob

4. What did Esau sell to his brother Jacob (Gen. 25:29-34)?

   _____ a. stew   _____ b. birthright _____ c. goat

5. Who was the wife of Isaac (Gen. 29:28)?

   _____ a. Sarah   _____ b. Rebekah   _____ c. Rachel

6. What festival celebrates God passing over the Israelites while in Egypt (Gen. 12:11)?

   _____ a. Pentecost _____ b. Passover   _____ c. Hanukah

7. Which of Jesus' disciples walked on water (Matt. 14:29)?

   _____ a. Peter   _____ b. Paul   _____ c. John

Fun Time #4

Across

3. Shared the fruit with her husband
6. To turn away from the sin
7. Took the punishment for our sins
9. When God forgets about our mistakes

Down

1. We need to _____ our parents
2. Someone to help us be a Christian
4. Tell God what you did wrong
5. You should do this after you are saved
8. Not doing what God tells you to do

PART V
My Challenges as a Christian

Chapter 25
I'm Saved, but I Keep Sinning

Is it okay to sin and just ask for forgiveness? Absolutely not! The Bible tells us that God expects us to obey Him. When we sin, we are disobeying God. God tells us that those who love Him will obey His Word. So it is not okay to keep doing bad things.

When the Holy Spirit comes to live within us, He whispers to us to do the right thing. We continue to do bad things, because we do not listen to the Holy Spirit. When we go to church regularly and read the Bible, we encourage the Holy Spirit to talk to us. You have to read the Bible to know what God wants you to do.

Samantha's teacher would tell the class every day to open their language books and read the instructions and complete the assignment. Samantha always wanted to be the first to complete her assignment, so she would skip the instructions. She was a very smart girl, so she couldn't understand why she always got a lot of the questions wrong.

After about a week of this, the teacher pulled her aside. She told Samantha that she must read the instructions. Samantha needed to stop thinking that she knew how to complete the assignment.

Sometimes we are like Samantha. We need to read God's instructions. Many Christians go through life without knowing what God considers a sin. By studying the Bible we will know what is not

My Child's Heart

pleasing to God. When we know this, the Holy Spirit can remind us of what we have read.

God's words in the Bible are so powerful that just by reading them we can stop sinning.

We must do everything we can to stop sinning. Sin only leads to bad consequences. *"Our Lord and our God, you answered their prayers and forgave their sins, but when they did wrong, you punished them"* (Ps. 99:8, CEV). So the consequence of sin is punishment. Adam and Eve were kicked out of the wonderful Garden of Eden and had to work hard for their food because they sinned.

My daughter can never keep track of her belongings. I have to buy replacements often because she misplaces everything. This is poor stewardship. *Stewardship* means taking care of things that have been given to you. On her birthday, she received a gift from her friend that she had been wanting. That week she wore the gift to school and lost it. I told her that God may have allowed her to lose something that is precious to her, because she is careless with the things that He gives her. I told her that she needs to ask God to forgive her for her lack of responsibility and poor stewardship. God punishes us in strange ways. He has a lot more power and control over things than your parents. This is why you should obey Him.

We can defeat sin with the help of the Holy Spirit. The Holy Spirit is our helper. That little voice that tells you not to do something is the Holy Spirit. So listen when that little voice speaks.

Sin is going against God's Word. Sin breaks God's heart!

I'm Saved, but I Keep Sinning

Think About It

Parent/Teacher:

- Talk about some of the mistakes you made this week. Discuss how people will make mistakes but must admit them and not hide like Adam and Eve.

Children:

- What did you learn about God?
- Does everybody make mistakes?
- How should you feel when you make a mistake?

    _____ a. That you are a horrible person

    _____ b. That this is wrong but God will forgive you

    _____ c. That sinning is okay

Key Verse

Anyone, then, who knows the good he ought to do and doesn't do it, sins.

(James 4:17, NIV)

Prayer Time

Dear God, help me be obedient to you always and to understand that when I am not obedient I will be punished. Amen.

Chapter 26
The Tricks of the Devil

Let's get back to our Bible story about Adam and Eve and learn why they ate from the forbidden tree. "*The serpent was clever, more clever than any wild animal GOD had made. He spoke to the Woman: 'Do I understand that GOD told you not to eat from any tree in the garden?' The Woman said to the serpent, 'Not at all. We can eat from the trees in the garden. It's only about the tree in the middle of the garden that GOD said, "Don't eat from it; don't even touch it or you'll die."' The serpent told the Woman, 'You won't die. GOD knows that the moment you eat from that tree, you'll see what's really going on. You'll be just like GOD, knowing everything, ranging all the way from good to evil.' When the Woman saw that the tree looked like good eating and realized what she would get out of it—she'd know everything!—she took and ate the fruit and then gave some to her husband, and he ate*" (Gen. 3:1-6, TM).

Satan's job is to trick us. He takes God's Word and twists it around. This is why God calls him clever. He told Eve an untruth about what would happen to her once she ate the fruit. She believed him over God. Don't fall into Satan's trap. Satan's tricks and traps are called "temptations" in the Bible. A temptation is an invitation to sin. He will tell you that God doesn't want you to have fun and that it is okay to lie so you won't get into trouble. He will tell you that you deserve to have a radio so go ahead and steal it or that you need to be perfect so cheat on your test. He will make you think that you are better than others, so it's okay to treat them unkindly. He will convince children that they can wait until they are adults to be saved. It is all a lie.

Adam and Eve were punished because they disobeyed God. He kicked them out of the wonderful Garden of Eden and told them life would be hard for them. God will punish us, even when we are tricked by Satan. This is why it is important for us to know the Word of God. By reading the Bible every day, we can fight against the ways of Satan. Satan's desire is to separate us from God. When we sin, we move further away from God.

Did You Know?

Satan wasn't always bad? He was one of God's angels. Satan wanted to be worshipped like God, so God kicked him out of heaven.

The Tricks of the Devil

God allows Satan to trick us, but He expects us to not give in. In fact, 1 Corinthians 10:13 cautions us that God will help us to not give in to Satan's tricks. With God on our side, we can always beat Satan. But we can only beat Satan when we listen to the Holy Spirit.

What types of tricks do you know? Here is a trick for fun.

Materials: Two quarters and a pen or marker

Description: The person you are tricking marks a coin and you place it in your right pocket. It magically jumps under your left foot.

Directions:

1. Take one of the quarters and mark an X on it.
2. Secretly place the extra quarter under your left foot. Have someone loan you a quarter, and ask them to mark it with an X.
3. Take the quarter, and just drop it into your right pant's pocket. Shake your leg as if you are shaking the coin into a hole and down your leg. Then say, "What's weird is that the hole isn't in this pocket, but in this one!" You lift up your other foot, and the coin is there!

This trick is only for fun and will not hurt anyone, but Satan's tricks hurt us.

THINK ABOUT IT

Parent/Teacher:

- Discuss a time when Satan tricked you.

Children:

- Where does temptation come from?
- What is temptation?

　　_____ a. Temptation is sin.

　　_____ b. Temptation is doing wrong.

　　_____ c. Temptation is an invitation to sin but is not sin.

- Discuss a time when Satan tricked you.
- Write down anything new that you have learned or want to remember.

Key Verse

But God can be trusted not to let you be tempted too much, and he will show you how to escape from your temptations.

(1 Cor. 10:13b, CEV)

Prayer Time

Dear God, help me know when Satan is trying to trick me. Help me run away from his temptations. Amen.

Chapter 27
We Are Selfish

We also sin because of our own selfish ways. We are born to just think about ourselves. People will tell you that it is all about you and that you should put yourself first. The Bible tells us that we should put others first. "*When tempted, no one should say, 'God is tempting me.' For God cannot be tempted by evil, nor does he tempt anyone; but each one is tempted when, by his own evil desire, he is dragged away and enticed. Then, after desire has conceived, it gives birth to sin; and sin, when it is full-grown, gives birth to death*" (James 1:13-15, NIV). We can not blame everything on Satan.

Jordan was watching television and enjoying herself when her brother entered the room. It was time for his favorite television show. Jordan knew before he asked that he wanted her to change the channel, but she pretended she didn't know why he was there. He finally said, "Hey, sis, can I change the channel?" She replied, "I am watching something right now." He went on to beg her, but she did not give in. Why do you think Jordan wouldn't let her brother watch his show? You are right if you said because she is selfish. Jordan was only thinking about herself. The Bible tells us that "*It's selfish and stupid to think only of yourself*" (Prov. 18:1a, CEV). Satan didn't tempt Jordan, she did this because she was only thinking

My Child's Heart

of herself. I can sometimes be selfish when it comes to food I like. When my children ask for something I am eating that I love, I don't want to share it with them. The Bible tells us that we should think about others first. So being selfish is not obeying God.

Jordan can stop being selfish by reminding herself every day that it is selfish and stupid to think only of herself.

If you are doing something now that you know is wrong or is a sin, please pray and ask God to help you stop. We have to make a choice whether to choose God's ways or Satan's ways. By focusing on God's Word, we can fight against our selfish ways.

We Are Selfish

Think About It

Parent/Teacher:

- When are you most selfish? Is this pleasing to God?
- Choose to serve one person in your family this week.

Children:

- *"And sin, when it is full grown, gives birth to death"* (James 1:14). What does death mean?

    _____ a. You will die.

    _____ b. You are separated from God.

- What does it mean to be selfish?
- What has Satan or your selfish desires told you to do that you know is wrong?
- Choose to do something kind for one person in your family this week.

Key Verse

It's selfish and stupid to think only of yourself.

(Prov. 18:1a, CEV)

Prayer Time

Dear God, please help me to put others before myself–especially my family. Amen.

Chapter 28
God Gives Us Tests Too

God also tests us to see if we are going to do the right thing. Tests are things that God allows to happen to us to test our faith. After your teacher teaches you certain things in math, she tests you to see how much you have learned. God tests us to see whether we are going to be obedient to Him. God gave Adam and Eve everything in the Garden of Eden to enjoy except the one tree of good and evil. They only had to trust God and respect His authority over them. God put that tree in the Garden of Eden to test Adam and Eve's loyalty and obedience to Him. Adam and Eve failed the test, because they ate the fruit. I want you to know that God did not cause Adam and Eve to sin. He put the tree there, but He did not encourage them to eat from it. He told them something bad would happen to them if they ate from the tree. God also tells us in the Bible that bad things will happen to us when we sin. Satan, on the other hand, told them something good would happen if they ate from the tree. Satan tempted them, and they gave in to the temptation.

God may give you an annoying sibling, but He does not make you treat your sibling unkindly. He may allow some children at school to be unkind to you, but He doesn't make you be unkind to them back. Only Satan will tell you to dislike someone or to

My Child's Heart

stay mad at someone for doing you wrong. When we are tested by God, He may allow someone to be unkind to us to see how we are going to respond. He wants to see if we are going to respond in kindness or listen to Satan. God will never tell us to do something that does not agree with the Bible.

God Gives Us Tests Too

Think About It

Parent/Teacher:

- Discuss a time when you could not understand why something was happening but you later saw God's plan develop.
- Share how God is testing you now.

Children:

- What did you learn about God?
- Can you think of ways that God may be testing you?
- Write down how God would like for you to respond to the test above.

Key Verse

Jesus replied, "If anyone loves me, he will obey my teaching."
(John 14:23a, NIV)

Prayer Time

Dear God, help me be obedient to your Word so that I may pass all of your tests. Amen.

Chapter 29
Why Do Bad Things Happen to Christians?

God will allow bad things (tribulations) to happen to us:

- To bring us closer to Him.
- To allow us to share our experiences with others so they can come to know Christ.

"As Jesus walked along, he saw a man who had been blind since birth. Jesus' disciples asked, 'Teacher, why was this man born blind? Was it because he or his parents sinned?' 'No, it wasn't!' Jesus answered. 'But because of his blindness, you will see God work a miracle for him. As long as it is day, we must do what the one who sent me wants me to do. When night comes, no one can work. While I am in the world, I am the light for the world.' After Jesus said this, he spit on the ground. He made some mud and smeared it on the man's eyes. Then he said, 'Go and wash off the mud in Siloam Pool.' The man went and washed in Siloam, which means 'One Who Is Sent.' When he had washed off the mud, he could see. The man's neighbors and the people who had seen him begging wondered if he really could be the same man. Some of them said he was the same beggar, while others said he only looked like him. But he told them, 'I am that man.' 'Then how can you see?' they asked. He answered, 'Someone named Jesus made some mud and smeared it on my eyes. He told me to go

My Child's Heart

and wash it off in Siloam Pool. When I did, I could see.' 'Where is he now?' they asked. 'I don't know,' he answered."

(John 9:1-12, CEV)

For every bad thing that happens to someone who is saved, God has a good reason for letting it happen. In the blind man's case, Jesus wanted others to see His powers and come to know that He is God. So many times when something bad happens to us, we cannot see the good in it. It is not until much later that we can see why God allowed something bad to happen.

After I graduated from college, I had a terrible car accident that almost killed me. I thought, *Why is this happening to me?* I was in the hospital for three weeks. It took me four months to learn to walk again. This was a very difficult time in my life. I had to rely on God to make it through. Jesus became my best friend after the car accident.

Why Do Bad Things Happen to Christians?

I told you that I was baptized at six years of age, but I didn't have a relationship with Christ until later. Life became so much better when Christ became my friend. I was able to talk to Him every day as often as I wanted and tell Him about my sadness. He gave me courage and peace. This was a bad accident for me and other people, but I would not change it because of my new friend Jesus.

This was a bad thing that God allowed to happen to me, but it turned out good! Bad things will happen to us and the people we love, but we need to trust that God knows better than us. If something is going on in your life that is painful, pray and ask God to help you deal with it and to give you peace. Nothing happens to us unless God lets it happen.

Think About It

Parent/Teacher:

- Tell about a time you trusted God and waited on Him.
- Was it hard to trust and wait on God?

Children:

- Discuss with your parents anything that is going on that is making you unhappy.
- What is the worst thing that has happened to you?
- What are some things that seem unfair to you?
- Do you think you have the right attitude about these things?

Key Verse

Wait for the Lord; be strong and take heart and wait for the Lord.
(Ps. 27:14, NIV)

Prayer Time

Dear God, I know that I might not understand why you allow bad and sad things to happen, but help me to trust you. Amen.

Chapter 30
Choose Today Whom You Will Serve

There was a boy who had gone camping with his family. His father wanted the family to experience what it would be like without all the wonderful things that we have today. He chose a campsite that didn't have any bathrooms, no cabins, and no other people around. The family brought food and a tent. They didn't even bring their cell phones.

When they were out on a hike one day, the son fell into a deep hole. The mother panicked and jumped in to save him but couldn't climb out. The father remembered that he had seen another family about 30 minutes away from them, so he headed out to find this family. But when he got to the location, they were gone. The sister remembered they had a rope, so she threw it down to the mother, but it was too short.

No one was around to save the mother and son. This is how it is with us. We cannot save ourselves, and no one else can either. Only God can save us. God can reach right into that hole and pull you out.

God loves sinners such as you and me. As sinners, we must choose to be saved by accepting Jesus Christ as our Lord and Savior. When Jesus is Lord over your life, you will do what He commands in the Bible.

I received a *religion* at the age of six, but I did not have a relationship with Jesus Christ until I was 21 years old. I am writing this book so you will not make the same mistake I made. You are never too young to accept Jesus Christ. No one knows when he or she is going to die or when Christ is coming again.

If you are not saved, you will not be able to go with Him. Be ready, get saved today!

God loves us and has written an awesome love letter to us in the Bible. He tells us that He knows everything about us, even the number of hairs on our heads. He wants to be close to us. He is our Father, He loves us very much, this is why He sent Jesus to die for us. He is only waiting for us to say yes to Him and no to our sinful ways. It is all up to us!

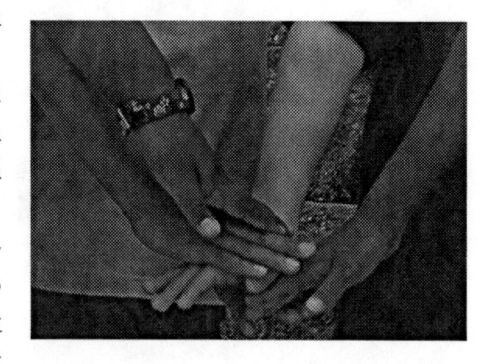

Be blessed, and I look forward to seeing you in heaven.

Kathy Kirk

Choose Today Whom You Will Serve

Commitment Contract

Thank you, Jesus, for dying on the cross for me. I know I am not worthy. I understand today that salvation is given to me freely. All I have to do is to believe in my heart that Jesus Christ died on the cross to forgive my sins. I must confess my sins and stop doing them. I also must invite Christ into my heart and be obedient to God's Word. I accept your free gift of salvation.

I will, from this day forward, concentrate on saying yes to you and no to sin. Today, I commit myself to you and to learning more about you. I will study your Word to learn more about you and what you expect from me. Please help me keep my commitment. Please help me do this all of my life. Amen.

_____   _____
Name   Date

Play It Again #5

Check how you should respond to each test below.

1. Brother hits you

    _____ a. Tell brother that this is not a loving thing to do, and God said we should love one another.

    _____ b. Hit brother back.

    _____ c. Ignore your brother all day.

2. Mother tells you to stop playing your game and go to bed.

    _____ a. Ignore mother and continue to play game.

    _____ b. Whine about having to go to bed.

    _____ c. Stop your game and go to bed.

3. Friend says something mean to you.

    _____ a. Say something mean back to your friend.

    _____ b. Stop playing with your friend.

    _____ c. Share with your friend how this makes you feel.

4. How should you deal with the painful things in your life?

    _____ a. Be mad at God.

    _____ b. Stop talking to God.

    _____ c. Pray to God for help and peace.

    _____ d. Be unkind to others.

Choose Today Whom You Will Serve

5. Adam and Eve had everything. Why do you think they sinned?

6. Why do bad things happen to Christians?

7. What are the consequences of sin for Christians?

8. What must a person do to be saved?

9. Why shouldn't people wait until they are adults to be saved?

BIBLE QUIZ #5

1. After Noah and his family entered the ark, how many days did it rain (Gen. 7:12)?

   _____ a. 60   _____ b. 45   _____ c. 40

2. When Jesus was crucified, how many other men were also crucified (Matt. 27:38)?

   _____ a. 4   _____ b. 2   _____ c. 1

3. Who lost his strength when his hair was cut (Judges 16:18-20)?

   _____ a. Samson   _____ b. Goliath   _____ c. Joseph

4. Who had a colorful coat (Gen. 37:3)?

   _____ a. Joseph   _____ b. David   _____ c. Isaac

5. What was Moses carrying when he came down from the mountain (Exod. 32:15)?

   _____ a. The Bible   _____ b. Ten Commandments

6. Who was the righteous man who built the ark (Gen. 6:9)?

   _____ a. Adam   _____ b. David   _____ c. Noah

7. How many times did Jesus say Peter would deny him (Matt. 26:34)?

   _____ a. 3   _____ b. 2   _____ c. 1

Choose Today Whom You Will Serve

8. How many brothers did Joseph have (Genesis 49:3,5,8,13,14,16,19,20,21,27)?

    _____ a. 15   _____ b. 4   _____ c. 11   _____ d. 9

My Child's Heart

Fun Time #5

Across

1. Your _____ have authority over you
4. He created everything
5. To tell God that what you have done is wrong
7. The only way to God (hint: Begins with a "s")
8. We are all _____
9. Not doing what God tells us to do

Down

2. God's _____ are to protect us
3. We are never too _____ to be saved
5. _____ friends help you to be obedient
6. _____ in the Lord Jesus and you will be saved

Choose Today Whom You Will Serve

Fun Time #5 (cont.)

Find the hidden words

Y	T	D	V	A	L	R	B	T	N	P	O	S	A	R
F	T	E	G	G	Z	A	Y	W	I	H	C	G	U	E
F	I	V	N	I	B	X	X	D	R	R	W	S	E	P
N	W	A	D	E	A	D	M	W	R	L	I	V	M	E
S	E	S	U	C	O	N	F	E	S	S	E	P	J	N
O	P	R	D	K	B	E	H	L	T	I	S	F	S	T
O	U	O	D	H	U	F	L	S	L	U	H	Z	K	F
E	D	K	S	L	F	S	U	E	E	K	D	V	W	C
F	T	Q	N	R	I	R	B	Z	Z	Y	F	J	W	Q
Q	C	E	I	X	T	H	X	X	I	N	M	Z	I	G
C	U	E	R	H	I	G	C	L	T	K	U	I	C	L
S	N	N	B	N	J	B	O	P	P	S	E	Q	B	S
D	B	R	E	Y	A	R	P	D	A	E	T	S	F	O
N	O	I	T	A	V	L	A	S	B	I	J	N	B	N
L	L	K	E	Y	M	T	C	Q	I	T	T	B	I	G

BAPTIZE ETERNAL SALVATION
BELIEVE FRIEND SAVED
CHILDREN GOD SON
CONFESS PRAYER SPIRIT
DEAD REPENT TRUST

Answer Key

Play It Again #1	Bible Quiz #1	Fun Time #1
1. God	1. 7,2,4,6,1,3,5	**Unscramble Names**
2. Yes	2. B	Noah, Joseph, Adam, David, Seth, Matthew, Jacob.
3. C	3. False	
4. Yes	4. Yes	
5. B		
6. Father, Son, Holy Spirit		

Fun Time #1 section continued:

Hidden Words

```
S + + + + S E S P E C I A L +
+ E + + P + V G + + + + + +
+ + L I + + E N + + + + + +
+ + R B + + + O + + + + + Y
B I + + A + + L + + + + T +
T A + + + T + E + + + + I + +
+ + R + + + E B + + + N + + +
+ + + R + + + G + H I + + + C
G + + + E + + + E R T + + + R
S O + + + N + + T V + R + + E
U + D + + + + + + + + A S A
S A D A M D L R O W + + R E T
E R E H W Y R E V E + A + + E
J + + + + + + + + + T + + + +
+ + + + + + + + + + S + + + +
```

My Child's Heart

Play It Again #2
1. C, 4. B, 5. A, 6. The Bible
	Bible Quiz #2
	1. A, 2. C, 3. Angel and flaming sword, 4. B
		Fun Time #2
		Unscramble the Bible Verse
		The wise of heart will receive commands but a babbling fool will be ruined.
		
		Hidden Words
		`G + + E U + t + + H + J + + +`
		`N + + C + N + + A + E + + + S`
		`I + S N + + K T + A + G + S +`
		`Y + S E + + I I L + N + E + +`
		`L C E I + N + O N I + N + + +`
		`G O N D G R U + T D H + + + +`
		`O V I E + S + H + S N + + + +`
		`S E Z B Y + G N I L A E T S +`
		`S T A O + I + F + + + + S + +`
		`I I L S F + L + + + + + + S +`
		`P N E I + + C H E A T I N G +`
		`I G + D S T U B B O R N E S S`
		`N + + + I + + Y R G N A + + +`
		`G + + + + R + + + + + + + + +`
		`+ + + + + + P + + + + + + + +`

Play It Again #3 1. C, 2. D, 3. B, 4. B	**Bible Quiz #3** 1. C, 2. A, 3. Holy Spirit, 4. 6, 7th, 5. They ate from the forbidden tree, 6. eternal life	**Fun Time #3** **Matching Letters** Believe that Jesus is Lord **Unscramble** This is love that we walk in obedience to his commands. **Salvation** Sat, sail, lion, son, ton, salt, not, lot, as, an, ant, last, list, lost, vast, sit, sin, saliva, lava, tin, tan

Answer Key

Play It Again #4 1. Jesus, 2. C, 3. A, 4. C, 5. Confess, 6. So God will forgive you.	Bible Quiz #4 1. B, 2. B, 3. C, 4. B, 5. B, 6. B, 7. A	Fun Time #4 Across 3. Eve, 6. Repent, 7. Jesus, 9. Mercy Down 1. Obey, 2. Mentor, 4. Confess, 5. Baptize, 8. Sin
| Play It Again #5<br>1. A, 2. C, 3. C, 4. C, 5. Selfish, 6. To bring you closer to God or so other people will get to know God, 7. Punishment, 8. Believe that Jesus Christ is Lord; confess sins and repent; make Jesus Lord over your life; and be obedient, 9. You may die as a child or Jesus may come back before you are an adult. | Bible Quiz #5<br>1. C, 2. B, 3. A, 4. A, 5. B, 6. C, 7. A, 8. C | Fun Time #5<br>Cross Word Puzzle<br>Across<br>1. Parents, 2. God, 3. Confess, 7. Salvation, 8. Sinners, 9. Sin<br>Down<br>2. Rules, 3. Young, 5. Christian, 6. Believe<br><br>**Hidden Words**<br><br>```
+ + D + + + + T + + + + R
+ + E + + + + + I + + + E
+ + V + + + + + R + + E P
N + A D E A D + + + I V + E
+ E S + C O N F E S S E P + N
+ + R + + + + + T I + + S T
+ + + D + + + S L + + + +
E + + L F + U E E + + + +
+ T + + R I R B + Z + + + +
+ + E I + T H + + I + + + +
+ + E R + + G C + T + + + +
+ N + + N + + O + P + + + S
D + R E Y A R P D A + + + O
N O I T A V L A S B + + + N
+ + + + + + + + + + + + + +
``` |
```

Remember to checkout our website for frequently asked questions by children, group discussion questions, and the following upcoming "My Child's Heart" books:

Salvation Starts In The Heart
What Goes In Must Come Out
My Friends And Siblings Are Driving Me Crazy
I Don't Like Being Told What To Do
The World Looks Good To Me

How to Reach Us

For more information, visit our "My Child's Heart" website! Log on to www.MyChildsHeart.org to discover new resources, sample group discussion, activities, and questions and ideas to help you and your child develop a life that is pleasing to God.

Pleasant Word

To order additional copies of this title call:
1-877-421-READ (7323)
or please visit our web site at
www.pleasantwordbooks.com

If you enjoyed this quality custom published book,
drop by our web site for more books and information.

www.winepressgroup.com
"Your partner in custom publishing."